All About IELTS

How the test works and **what you need to do** to get a good grade

Fiona Aish and Jo Tomlinson

© Prosperity Education Ltd. 2022

Registered offices: Sherlock Close, Cambridge
CB3 0HP, United Kingdom

First published 2022

ISBN: 978-1-913825-67-6

This publication is in copyright. Subject to statutory exception
and to the provisions of relevant collective licensing agreements,
no reproduction of any part may take place without the written
permission of Prosperity Education.

'IELTS' is a brand belonging to Cambridge Assessment English,
the British Council and IDP: IELTS Australia, and is not associated
with Prosperity Education or its products.

The moral rights of the authors have been asserted.

Cover design by ORP Cambridge

For further information and resources, visit:
www.prosperityeducation.net

To infinity and beyond.

Contents

Introduction	4
1. All about the test	5
2. Listening	11
3. Speaking	29
4. Reading	40
5. Writing	55
Appendix 1 – Listening: Audio download and transcripts	73
Appendix 2 – Reading text: The Unluckiest Astronomer in the World?	77
Appendix 3 – Writing: Other types of visual information	79
Glossary & index	84
IELTS Academic Reading Practice: exemplar content and sample paper	88

Introduction
All About IELTS

Who is this book for?

This book is for advanced speakers of English and first-language English speakers who wish to take the IELTS Academic test and want to find out more about what the exam entails, and, importantly, how to take the test effectively. Unlike many other IELTS books, it is not a coursebook, and it does not include language practice. Rather, it includes information about the test format, what is being tested and how you can give good answers in the test.

The book is separated into five main chapters: the first section gives an overview of the exam, and the subsequent chapters look at each part of the test. The second chapter focuses on the Listening test, the third the Speaking test, the fourth the Reading test, and then, lastly, the Writing test. You do not have to read the chapters in order if you do not want to. Each chapter contains test information and exam tips. You also have an option to practise the question and task types.

As much as possible, this book utilises accessible language. Certain grammatical terms and more-technical language are linked to an indexed glossary on pages 84–87.

Audio files for the chapter on Listening can be downloaded by following the instructions on page 73.

About the authors

Fiona Aish has co-written several titles in exam preparation and EAP, and creates materials and assessment resources for a range of educational providers. She is DELTA-qualified and holds an MA in ELT and Applied Linguistics.

Jo Tomlinson has co-written a number of books on EAP and exam preparation, and currently works full-time as an exams and materials developer. She is DELTA-qualified and holds an MA in Language Testing.

Fiona and Jo are directors of Target English, a consultancy in Spain that provides tailor-made solutions in content creation, course provision, training and testing.

Chapter 1
All about the test

The IELTS exam

The International English Language Testing System (IELTS) is one of the world's most popular tests of English **proficiency** and is commonly used for people who want to study in English or move to English-speaking countries. If you are about to take IELTS, it is essential that you find out what you need to do. Remember, English language knowledge is only one part of the test, and knowing the test can have an impact on the score you get. When taking any exam, you need to be as calm and in control as possible. This means limiting any surprises and finding out what you've got to do and how you're going to do it ahead of time.

This section gives an overview of the IELTS Academic test, outlines what the scores mean, and offers some insight on why the exam is the way it is. It will also explore some specific problems you might have with the exam. If you feel you already know the exam format very well, you could move straight to the skills sections (chapters 2–5).

An overview

There are two types of IELTS test: General and Academic. This book focuses on IELTS Academic. The test is in four parts: Listening, Speaking, Reading and Writing. Testing is normally carried out over two separate days. The listening, reading and writing components are completed in that order on the same day, while the speaking component will be assessed within seven days (before or after) the other components. At the time of writing, the test is still done on paper rather than on a computer, so you will need to hand-write your answers. Here is a brief outline of the parts of the test:

Listening	Speaking	Reading	Writing
30 minutes (plus 10 minutes to transfer answers)	11–14 minutes	60 minutes	60 minutes
4 sections	3 sections	3 texts	2 tasks
40 questions	Questions about yourself; longer speaking task; discursive questions	40 questions	Summary of visual information (150 words); and an essay (250 words)

Listening test

In the Listening test, you will hear four recordings, and they usually get more difficult as you continue through the sections. When listening, you need to answer questions that check you understand what you hear, and you will only hear the recordings once. The listening section is 30 minutes long, with an extra ten minutes at the end of the recordings to transfer your answers onto the answer paper. There are 40 questions in total, and the question types will vary.

The first recording is a simple **transactional** conversation, such as booking a hotel or course, and the second recording is a **monologue** about something that is general in topic, such as a tour guide explaining the sights in the city. The third and fourth recordings are on more academic themes. In the third recording, you will hear people discussing something educational, for example students discussing a class project. In the final recording, you will hear another monologue that is more similar in style to a lecture.

Speaking test

The Speaking test is 11–14 minutes long, and is, at the time of writing, done face to face with two examiners (one will speak to you, and the other will assess your English). The test will also be recorded.

This test is in three parts. In part one, the examiner will ask you general questions about yourself (this could be about your home town, job, reasons for learning English, etc.). This will last for about 4–5 minutes.

The second part is called an 'individual long turn'. As the name suggests, you will have to speak on a subject alone for 1–2 minutes. You will be given a topic card that will tell you what you need to speak about, and you will have a minute to prepare what you are going to say. In the preparation time, you can write notes on your answer. The examiner will end this part by asking one or two questions once you have spoken.

In the final part, you will be asked questions relating to the topic in Part 2, but these will be of a more **discursive** or **abstract** nature. So, for example, if you have talked about a journey in Part 2, Part 3 could be about the problems of air pollution, or the effects of tourism. This will last for about 4–5 minutes.

Chapter 1 – All about the test

Reading test

Unlike the Listening test, the Reading test doesn't significantly increase in difficulty, and the passages have no distinct features like the structure of the listening test. You will have three long passages (in total around 2,500 words) and 40 questions to answer about these passages. Like the Listening test, the question types vary for this component. The reading section is 60 minutes long, and you'll need to write your answers down on the answer paper within these 60 minutes.

Exam Tip: If English is your first language, this could be the paper you need to focus on the most. This is simply because it is perhaps a different way of reading than you are used to. You do not have a lot of time to read the text and answer the questions, so it is better to focus on reading the questions and finding the answers, rather than reading the text and then reflecting on the answers.

If you can, practise doing timed tests before your exam.

Writing test

The Writing test is 60 minutes long and contains two sections. The first task is a description of visual information. This should be at least 150 words. The kind of visual information you need to describe can vary. For example, it could be a graph, pie chart, or map.

The second task is an essay in which you will need to state your opinion and give reasons for your opinion. You should write at least 250 words for this task.

Exam Tip: The second task is worth more marks than the first task, so try to spend 20 minutes on Task 1 and 40 minutes on Task 2.

Scoring

The scores are given in 'bands'. The score range is from 0 to 9, and you can score half bands too (e.g. between a 5.0 and a 6.0 is 5.5). You will get a score for each part of the test and then an overall score. 0 is the lowest score and is given when a candidate does not attempt any answers. 9 is the highest score and equates with an expert or fluent user.

Generally, to get onto an undergraduate degree programme, candidates need to aim for 5.5 or 6.0. However, this will depend on the university and the subject. For master's degrees or for visas for positions in areas such as nursing, test takers will be required to get a 7.0 or higher in all parts. Again, courses and universities differ in their entrance requirements, so you need to check this.

Band scores relate to the following levels of proficiency, from Band 5 upwards:

Band 5	**Modest user** – partial command of English, likely to make many mistakes.
Band 6	**Competent user** – effective command of the language with some misunderstanding.
Band 7	**Good user** – generally strong operational command of English.
Band 8	**Very good user** – full operational command of English with occasional errors.
Band 9	**Expert user** – full operational command of English.

You are given a band score for each of the four sections. Your overall score is the rounded average of the four sections. For example:

Listening score: 6.5   Reading score: 7   Speaking score: 5.5   Writing score: 5.5

Average score: 6.125
Overall band score: 6

Detailed information about the IELTS test format and scoring system can be found online at www.ielts.org.

The most important thing to understand about the scores is what you need and what you need to do to get that score.

Some reasoning behind the examination

There are many reasons why the examination is designed as it is. Firstly, there are reasons of practicality and reliability. There are lots of test takers in many different parts of the world, so the test needs to be delivered in different contexts, yet the results need to be meaningful. In terms of the Reading and Listening papers, having question papers with set answers means that there is little deviation between individuals (just right or wrong answers), and everyone is being assessed in the same way.

The examination makes efforts to be as fair as possible for all test takers. This means that sometimes the readings are on unusual subjects, but this is better than focusing on more-familiar subjects that some candidates might know but others are not familiar with. For example, imagine if a reading text was about pop music in China. A lot of test takers from China might be able to answer the questions more easily because they are probably more familiar with the subject. This is exactly why subjects are chosen to be accessible, but not focus on existing knowledge of candidates.

The examination also tests the skills that are needed at university. We will look more in-depth at what each part of the test is testing in later sections, but for now let's look at this in general. The Reading test requires you to process and understand details in quite long texts in a short amount of time. This is something you're likely to do at university. There you will have a lot to read, and you'll need to read effectively and understand key points. In terms of the Writing test, the sections are quite different, but this is an indication that you can write both factually and deal with data that may appear in reports as well as present an argument, which is commonly required when writing essays.

How well will I do?

This depends on your level of English but also how familiar you are with the examination. However, there is one important thing to remember: there is no way to 'beat' the test. Knowing the format helps, but you need vocabulary, grammar and the skills of reading, writing, listening and speaking at the appropriate level.

There will be parts of each paper that you are better at, and parts that you find more difficult. As previously mentioned, often for first language English speakers, the Reading test is the most difficult. For people whose first language isn't English, the parts you are good at may vary. Often, candidates can get the scores they require in Reading and Listening, but not in Writing and Speaking.

Exam Tip: Probably the most important question here is: how do you know what parts you need to improve and how can you improve them?

Firstly, do a practice test. There are tests on the official IELTS website. Check your answers and your scores, and you will realise the areas in which you may require additional preparation. However, with your Writing and Speaking practice, ask someone who has a higher level of English than you to check your performance because this is impossible for a book to assess adequately.

Once you have an idea of your performance in each part, you can start practising to improve the skills you need. For example, if Listening is your weakest skill, you might want to focus more on this area by listening to English radio programmes or online lectures (possibly with subtitles), or by buying a preparation book that focuses on this skill.

Chapter 2
Listening

Listen tactically

Listening tests are not very similar to how you normally listen because they are designed to check how well you can listen to English language. You might be somebody who enjoys listening to the radio or having conversations with people. You might think these activities make you a good listener, but for this test, being a good listener is quite different. In the Listening test, you'll be doing four things at once: reading, thinking, listening *and* writing. This is not something that most people are used to doing. To do well in IELTS Listening, you need to be able to listen more tactically. Let's have a look at how your reading skills can help you in the listening component.

Firstly, you need to read the question paper. Start by reading the instructions for each set of questions. You may think this is obvious, but many people lose marks just because they haven't read and followed the instructions. We'll look at the specific question types later, but, generally, you may be asked to answer some questions or complete some sentences. To do this, you need to read and understand the questions or sentences, and know what you are listening for. It's best to do this by finding some of the more unusual words (this is often more technically called '**low-frequency vocabulary**') in the questions and by finding out what kind of answer you need. Let's look at three examples:

1 How many flights does John need to take?
2 The most difficult part of the presentation was the _____.
3 Mars was known by _____ astronomers In around the 4th century BCE.

Let's start by focusing on the most unusual words. These are the ones that when you hear them, you might hear the answer nearby. So, for example, in Question 1 above there is no need to listen for 'to'. It's a word that you're going to hear a lot. The words here that indicate when the answer is going to come are 'John' and 'flights'. Let's explore this further: what if the audio is all about John booking flights? (You can usually tell this by looking at the other questions in that group of questions.) Well, then these unusual words aren't going to help you much. Then, you also need to look at what information you need, and we can find this out from the question. In Question 1 above, the information needed is in the question words 'How many' – so here you are looking for a number of flights. Now, try to think of what the unusual words are, and what type of information you need to know to answer Questions 2 and 3 before you continue reading.

The second example (Question 2) is a little more difficult. Perhaps the whole audio will be about the presentation, so that's not much help. The key here is 'most difficult part' – that's essentially what you are listening for. Also, the answer is going to be a noun. You can tell this because 'the' precedes the space. You might need an adjective and noun, but you will definitely need a **noun**.

The third example (Question 3) is a little different because here you've got lots of unusual words. So, you could listen for 'Mars', 'astronomers' and 'the 4th century BCE'. This is where it is important to look at all the other questions. Each section is on a particular subject, so if Mars is mentioned in most of the questions, look at the other words instead. This will help you pinpoint the answer.

Now let's look at Question 3 and determine what kind of answer we need. If you read the sentence without the gap, the sentence makes sense. This indicates that the information in the space is giving more detail. Words that add detail are usually **adjectives** and **adverbs**. In this case, we are looking for an adjective. In fact, we're looking for a type of astronomer.

This is how, using the questions given on the paper, reading can help your listening. Some of the later sections in this chapter will also explore how thinking and writing are involved in listening.

It gets harder

There are four sections in the Listening test, and, usually, the sections are increasingly difficult. As briefly mentioned in the introduction to this book, the first two sections are based on general English speaking:

- You will hear a **transactional** dialogue in the first section. In our experience there are only so many things you can have a transactional dialogue about. The most common types are: booking a holiday/journey/course; finding information about a holiday/journey/course; and buying a meal/clothes/books. So, you should be able to prepare for this by learning about using English in these kinds of scenarios. The questions are also quite factual: they are usually asking for times, names, and facts.

- The second section is harder to predict subject-wise. It's a **monologue** (one person speaking) about something general in topic. This really could be anything; topics that *could* appear include the opening of a sports centre, a tour, and film reviews among other things. So, this section is more difficult to prepare for.

The third and fourth sections are more academic in nature:

- The third section involves a discussion. This could be among students or among students and their tutor. It could be something such as a meeting to discuss a project or presentation. The questions are also a little more difficult. They can be less based on simple facts and more on understanding discussion or opinion.

- The last section is similar to a lecture. You will hear one person speak on a subject, and you have to answer questions about this. Again, these questions are not likely to be about names, times or factual information, but about understanding the themes and details of the lecture.

Exam Tip: There is no way of knowing what question types you will get with each section. They change. There is a set list of question types, which we shall look at later, but you will not know when a particular question type might appear. The questions are spread evenly throughout: each section has ten questions.

Don't get distracted

You might think by *distracted*, we mean not to let your attention wander from the test, but actually **distraction** here applies to the test. Some question types have right and wrong options. The wrong options are known as **distractors**. The IELTS Listening test can have quite a lot of distraction (especially at the beginning). Let's look at an example. Imagine you hear this:

> There are many amenities in our sports centre. We've not only got tennis courts, but we've also got an Olympic-size swimming pool at your disposal. We're soon to be building a day-care centre for children so you can exercise in peace too!

Let's look at a typical question:

1 What facility doesn't the sports centre have at the moment?

    A Tennis court

    B Crèche

    C Full-size pool

All About IELTS

The distraction is in the language. You sometimes directly hear the other options (in this case 'tennis court' and 'pool'), but you do not directly hear the correct answer ('crèche'). In the audio they have used the words 'day-care centre', which means the same as 'crèche'. Also look at the language surrounding the wrong answers in the question; near 'tennis court' is the word 'not', and near 'pool' is the word 'disposal', so these might make you think one of these is the right answer when in fact both of them are not. Be careful of this in the test – listen for the *right* answer, not just the first thing you hear.

The two question types

In truth, there are more than two question types, but we can group them into two categories: **completion questions** and **selection questions**. Before we look at these in more detail, there is one important thing to mention again: read the instructions! You need to do this for each group of questions. This will tell you how you need to answer the questions, and you need to pay attention to whether you have to write a letter, which you may need to do in a selection question, or a certain number of words, which is common in a completion question.

Here we will outline the question types, and at the end of this chapter, after you have read all the advice, you will be able to listen to short audio samples and try and answer some exam-styled questions.

Let's look at completion questions first. These are when you have to write the answers in words (rather than a letter or a number).

Completion questions

In all completion questions, you have to fill in a gap in the text. This is usually with up to three words and/or a number, but be sure to read the instructions because sometimes you may be restricted to just two words. The word or words must be from the audio, and you cannot change the words. You must write them when you hear them and use the same words as you hear on the audio. Remember, do not change the words – write exactly what you hear. Let's look at some completion questions:

1. Form completion

This type of question is self-explanatory: you need to complete details on a short form. The form is usually not in full sentences. You just need to make sure that you have the correct type of information for the gap.

Chapter 2 – Listening

An example might be:

Student Retail Form

Name: 1 _____ Peterson

Date of birth: 14.07.1998

Address: 110 2 _____. Brighton, England

Email: a.peterson@mail.uk

---

2. Sentence completion

This kind of question is also self-explanatory. You need to insert a word or words into a sentence. Remember, as with all completion questions you will be given a word count in the instructions. Here are a couple of examples:

1   Students must apply _____ in order to renew the rail card.
2   The rail card gives students a _____ on standard ticket prices.

3. Short answer questions

Short answer questions are a little different to most other questions. Here you will see a question, and you must answer it. It is different because there is no specific gap to fill. You just need a few words to answer the question. Remember, don't write full sentences.

1   How much is the student rail card per year? _____

4. Table completion

Table completion questions are just as they sound – you have to complete information in a table. You will need to look at the format to tell whether you need smaller words such as **articles**. Tables also give you a lot of clues about how the information is organised. For example, by looking at the table and the numbering of the following questions, you can see that the speaker will probably talk about each event in turn and mention the name, time, and location for each one.

All About IELTS

Event	Time	Location
1 _____ workshop	3.00 – 4.00pm	Studio
Practice your Shakespeare	12.30pm – 2 _____ pm	Main stage
Acting careers talk	2.30 – 4.00pm	3 _____

5. Note completion

Like the form and table completion questions, note completion questions usually don't use full sentences. This means that you can sometimes miss out a small word such as an article (i.e. 'a', 'an', 'the') in your answer, but be sure to look at the notes surrounding the spaces and copy the format (i.e. if the notes don't miss out an article, then you shouldn't).

> Meeting with Dr. Weber: Tuesday 10.00am
>
> Tell her project decision – Focus = an 1 _____ robot
>
> Problem = communication
>
> Target users = children with 2 _____
>
> To ask: suggestions on working out the 3 _____ of the robot

6. Summary completion

A summary completion question is probably one of the harder question types. Here you will have a **paragraph** of text, and you will need to complete the text with a word or words from the audio. There is a lot to do, because you need to read the summary and listen to the speaker talking while completing the spaces. For this question type, look at the grammar around the spaces. The summary will be written in complete sentences. You need to complete the spaces with the correct type of word (e.g. **noun/verb**), so the sentences are grammatically correct. These questions will not be in note form.

> Slang refers to the language which is used by people who share a 1 _____ Originally it is believed to have been used by 2 _____ to disguise their communication. However, in modern times slang brings all kinds of people together in groups. Slang is mostly produced by the influence of 3 _____ .

Chapter 2 – Listening

7. Flow chart completion

A flow chart usually describes a process (e.g. how to make cheese or how to apply for a job). Flow chart completion questions are very similar to table completion questions because a flow chart is quite visual, and so can guide you through the questions. Again, you need to complete the spaces with words you hear and with the correct number of words/numbers. Look at the words and phrases in the following chart to see if the language is in note form or in full sentences.

How lexicographers choose slang words for the dictionary

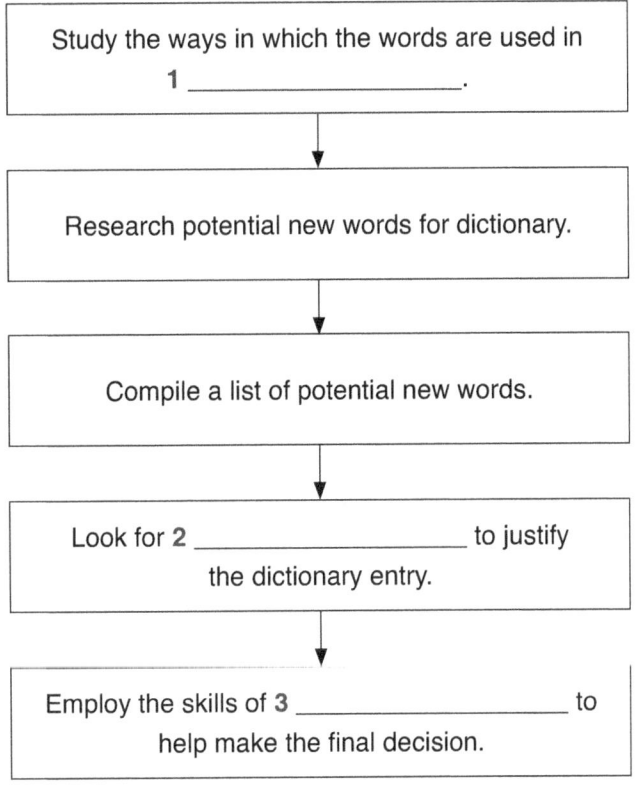

Selection questions

In selection questions, you have to choose a letter to write as your answer. You do not write the words in the answer on the answer sheet; you just write the letter, for example: A, B or C. Let's look at the selection question types:

All About IELTS

8. Multiple choice questions

You've undoubtedly come across these types of questions before. They are probably the most common exam question type, and are used in many exams throughout the world. You see a question or the beginning of a sentence, and you have to choose the option that is correct from a list of options. In the case of the Listening test, there are three answer options to chose from (A, B or C).

1   The student rail card cannot be used ...

   A   on national holidays.

   B   during rush-hour times.

   C   on airport express trains.

9. Matching

In matching questions, there are two lists of information, and you need to match the lists together. There might be a longer list of options in the box than needed to answer the questions. You need to use the same list of options for each question, and you may be able to use a letter more than once. Remember that the instructions will ask you to write the *letter* as your answer, not the information next to it. The best way of explaining this is with an example:

What are the students worried about on their courses? Match the students (**A–D**) to questions 1–3.

   A   Mark
   B   Jane
   C   Stephanie
   D   David

1   finding time to finish a project   _____
2   managing a large amount of reading   _____
3   getting organised for a large assignment _____

Chapter 2 – Listening

Completion or selection questions

There is one question type in this section: labelling a plan, map or diagram. You may see this as a completion question when you have to write the answers as words. Alternatively, if there is a box with a list of answers, this becomes a selection question because you write the letter from the options on the answer sheet. Here is an example:

10. Plan/Map/Diagram labelling

You will see a plan or map, or a picture or diagram, and you will need to label some features. There will be some features already labelled, and these will help guide you as you listen. Remember to read the instructions so you know if it is a completion or selection question.

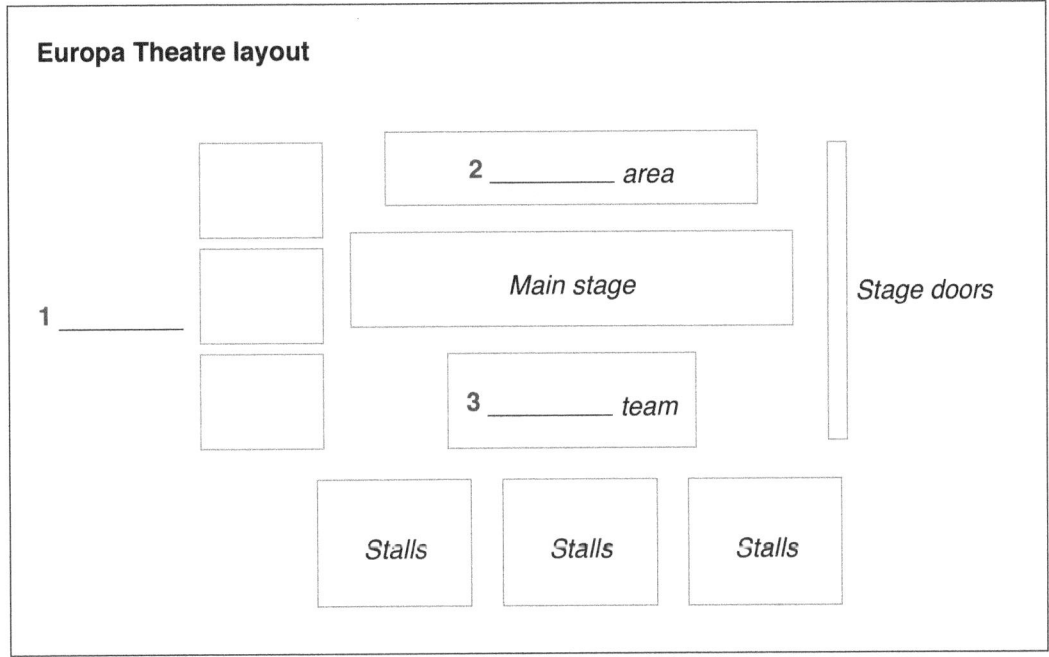

How paraphrasing works

Those are all the kinds of question types you might see in the Listening test. There will be two or three question types per section, and some may be repeated, so you'll have a mix of formats within the test. All of these question types involve some kind of **paraphrasing.**

All About IELTS

Paraphrasing is basically being able to express the same meaning in different ways using different language (grammar, structure, and vocabulary). Let's look at an example of how this works via a multiple-choice question:

1 Who was at the opening of the theatre?
   A   a famous actor
   B   a local official
   C   a member of the royal family

The audio might go a little like this:

> The Prince's Theatre has been open since 1798, and it has had a long reputation showing fine shows with many big-name actors in it. The ceremony to mark the first show was attended by the area's first mayor.

Look at how the *wrong* options are mentioned in a way that makes them almost plausible answers. We hear the word 'prince', and think of a member of a royal family; we hear the phrase 'big-name actor', and also we have the word 'open' ('has been open since…'), which makes us think the answer is coming because 'opening' is in the question. But these are distractions again. The paraphrase of the question 'Who was at the opening of the theatre?' is actually in this sentence: 'The ceremony to mark the first show was attended by the area's first mayor.' The 'opening' is paraphrased as 'the ceremony to mark the first show'; 'was at' becomes 'attended', and the grammar changes from **active** in the question to **passive** in the audio ('was attended'). The answer is also paraphrased. The 'local official' is the 'mayor'.

So, what does this tell you? Firstly, don't listen to simply match the words. You need to actively listen, and be aware that you are going to hear more than one option. Remember to listen for detail.

This is also true when it comes to completion questions. The same question, rewritten as a completion question, would be:

The 1 _____ of the town was at the opening of the theatre.

It works in a similar way, but we must write the answer from what we hear. So, here the answer would be 'first mayor'.

Chapter 2 – Listening

> **Exam Tip:** Be careful not to add information that is already in the sentence. We do not need to write 'areas' (which is in the audio) because 'of the town' gives us that information.

From a question design point of view, adding 'of the town' into the question makes the question very easy. The answer is unlikely to be 'prince' or 'famous actor' (which are mentioned in the audio) because it sounds strange next to 'The _____ of the town'. In terms of the 'actor', it makes us think that there is only one famous actor in the town; and a prince rarely is 'The prince of the town', rather of a country! Let's take it away:

The 1 _____ was at the opening of the theatre.

Here the answer could be 'area's first mayor', 'first mayor' or 'mayor'. The words 'area' and 'first' just give us more information; they are not necessary to have the correct answer. The **distractors**, also known as the wrong possible answers, become more plausible.

The important thing to think about is that the paraphrase is just the same here as for the multiple choice question. The only difference is that you don't have options to distract you, and you must write the answer from what you hear.

So, whether you are answering a completion question or a selection question, the listening questions and audio all involve some form of paraphrasing.

> **Exam Tip:** If you want to do well at IELTS, explore paraphrasing. It can be done grammatically or **lexically**, and it is fundamental to the Listening test.

Why listening to English can be difficult

Listening is sometimes the trickiest of the skills, simply because you don't just need to know the words, you also need to be able to recognise them (or a **paraphrase** of them) when you hear them, and be able to spell them. English is no fun in terms of its spellings and pronunciation. Rarely are words said in the way they are spelt.

All About IELTS

Let's take these 'ou' words as an example: thr<u>ou</u>gh, s<u>ou</u>thern, y<u>ou</u>r, h<u>ou</u>se. 'ou' has a different sound in each of those words, but *through* and *threw*, which are spelt completely differently, have an 'ou' sound which is exactly the same! This isn't the only problem: **connected speech** and **weak forms** can make listening even more difficult.

Connected speech is when words sound like they are joined together. This often happens in English speech, and is most common when one word starts or ends in a **vowel**. There are many different ways in which connected speech works. Let's explore some examples:

Take the sentence 'I'm the daughter of an English athlete.' It's easy to read, but what you might actually hear is something like this: 'I'm the daufterov van ninglish shathlete.'

 Listen to the audio: Athlete's Daughter (Page 73)

> Note here how the words 'daughter of an English athlete' all join together. The fact that natural speech in English often has these connections can make it especially difficult to understand.

Weak forms are when words lose their 'formal' pronunciation. We all know how 'and' sounds, but often in speech it is lost. Think of the 'and' in 'fish and chips'; it's actually like an 'n' sound – 'fish n chips'. It's quite common to reduce 'and' to 'n'. This is not the only example – this happens with smaller words such as 'been', 'of', 'can' and many other words. 'Been' can often sound like 'bin', 'can' sometimes sound like the 'a' disappears, and 'of' often loses the strong 'o' sound.

Unfortunately, there are no quick answers to solve such difficulties with listening. It does help to understand some of the reasons why it happens (such as the effect of connected speech or weak forms), but essentially to be a better listener, you need to listen more. If listening is a weakness, try listening to the radio in English or watching films or lectures in English. You can do this with subtitles to help you understand what is being said. Of course, as with anything in life you want to improve, you normally need to practise. This is especially true of listening.

Exam Tip: English accents vary a lot, and you might hear a mix of different speakers of English, perhaps Australian or Scottish, etc. Try to vary what you listen to so you can get used to different ways of speaking English.

The importance of spelling and grammar

Another key point to mention is the importance of grammar. This was touched upon in the section on listening tactically, but actually grammar can help you significantly in not only identifying answer types, but also in using the correct format. There will be words on the question sheet, and you can use these to help you. Let's look at a note completion example:

Files sent to factory.

1 _____ made for printer.

Copies sent to 2 _____.

Just by looking at the words surrounding the gaps, and using our knowledge of grammar, we can give ourselves an advantage when it comes to answering the question. Firstly, we know number 1 is going to be a noun, because a *thing* is made. We also know that we need to answer in note form because the structures are **passive** but do not include the verb 'to be'.

For example, the correct form for 'Files sent to' is 'The files are sent to'. This also tells us that we do not need to include 'is/are' in the answer. A wise person might suspect the question will be paraphrased by turning that passive structure to active, and they would listen out for this.

When we look at number 2, we can also work out that we probably need a **noun** and no **article** (e.g. 'customer' not 'the customer'). Things are usually sent to people or places, so we might be looking for a person or place.

That's how knowing grammar can help you with the questions. Not only can it indicate what kind of answers you need, it also can tell you how full grammatically those answers need to be.

Spelling is also important. If you misspell an answer, you will not get the points for it. So, think carefully about spelling the words and transferring words to the answer sheet. In Part 1, you might have to spell a name, so make sure you are familiar with how the letters sound in English.

Exam Tip: Make sure you understand the structure of a sentence and pay attention to what part of that structure is missing in the gaps. This helps you to identify what kind of word you need.

All About IELTS

Try the questions

There is no better way to understand how the question types work than to have a go at answering some. Look at the following questions, which you will recognise from the question type section. These questions and the accompanying audio recordings are small samples of each section for you to listen to (in the real test you will be listening to longer recordings, and there will be more questions). Try to answer these questions using the advice you have read in this section, and then refer to the answers that follow. Do not skip to the answers before you listen!

Sample section 1

 Listen to the audio: Section 1 (page 73)

Answer the question below. Write **NO MORE THAN TWO WORDS AND/OR A NUMBER**.

1 How much is the student rail card per year? £ _____

Complete the form below. Write **NO MORE THAN TWO WORDS AND/OR A NUMBER** for each answer.

Student Retail Form

Name: 2 _____ Peterson

Date of birth: 14. 07. 1998

Address: 110 3 _____. Brighton, England

Email: a.peterson@mail.uk

Complete the sentences below. Write **NO MORE THAN TWO WORDS AND/OR A NUMBER** for each answer.

4 Students must apply _____ in order to renew the rail card.

5 The rail card gives students a _____ on standard ticket prices.

Choose the correct letter, A, B or C.

6   The student rail card cannot be used ...

   A   on national holidays.

   B   during rush-hour times.

   C   on airport express trains.

Sample section 2

 Listen to the audio: Section 2 (page 74)

Complete the table below. Write **NO MORE THAN TWO WORDS AND/OR A NUMBER** for each answer.

Event	Time	Location
1 _____ workshop	3.00 – 4.00pm	Studio
Practise your Shakespeare	12.30pm – 2 _____ pm	Main stage
Acting careers talk	2.30 – 4.00pm	3 _____

Complete the plan below. Write **NO MORE THAN TWO WORDS AND/OR A NUMBER** for each answer.

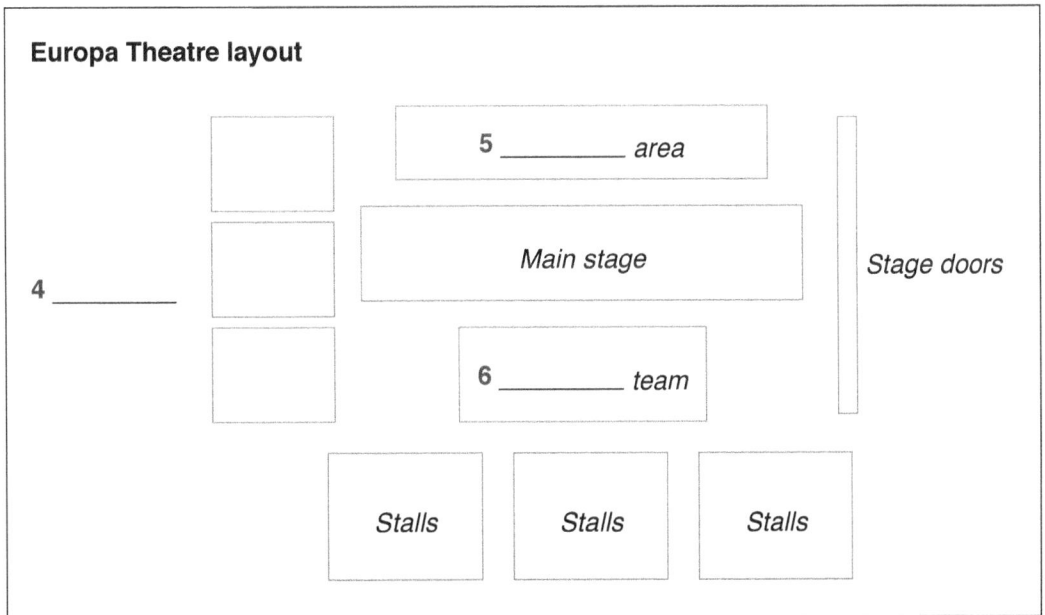

All About IELTS

Sample section 3

🎧 **Listen to the audio: Section 3 (page 75)**

Match the students (**A–D**) to questions **1–3**.

What are the students worried about on their courses? Match the students (**A–D**) to questions **1–3**.

> A Mark
> B Jane
> C Stephanie
> D David

1 finding time to finish a project   _____

2 managing a large amount of reading   _____

3 getting organised for a large assignment _____

Complete the notes below. Write **NO MORE THAN ONE WORD AND/OR A NUMBER** for each answer.

> Meeting with Dr. Weber: Tuesday 10.00am
>
> Tell her project decision – Focus = an **4** _____ robot
>
>   Problem = communication
>
>   Target users = children with **5** _____
>
> To ask: suggestions on working out the **6** _____ of the robot

Chapter 2 – Listening

Sample section 4

 Listen to the audio: Section 4 (page 76)

Complete the summary below. Write **NO MORE THAN ONE WORD AND/OR A NUMBER** for each answer.

Slang refers to the language which is used by people who share a
1 _____. Originally it is believed to have been used by
2 _____ to disguise their communication. However, in modern times slang brings all kinds of people together in groups. Slang is mostly produced by the influence of 3 _____.

Complete the flow chart below. Write **NO MORE THAN ONE WORD AND/OR A NUMBER** for each answer.

How lexicographers choose slang words for the dictionary

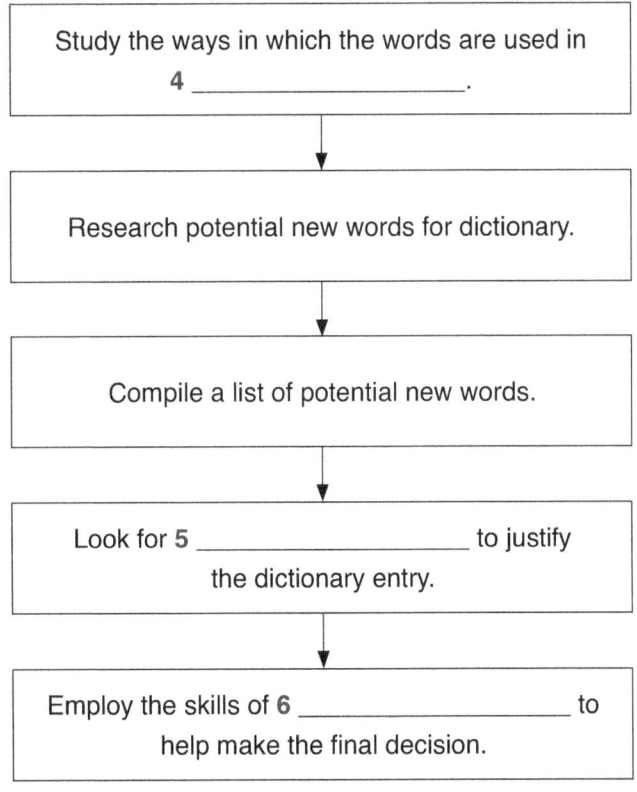

Answers

Remember, when you mark yourself, you must have the exact answers written here. Approximations are not acceptable. Also, you must have spelt every answer correctly.

Section 1	1. 36 / thirty six; 2. Adam; 3. Central Street; 4. online 5. 25% discount; 6. C
Section 2	1. costume design; 2. 1.30 / one thirty; 3. learning room; 4. dressing room; 5. changing; 6. sound production
Section 3	1. B; 2. C; 3. A; 4. educational; 5. disabilities; 6. price
Section 4	1. context; 2. criminals; 3. social forces; 4. everyday life; 5. evidence; 6. language experts

Further practice

Remember, the audio recordings in the real test will be much longer, but these exemplar questions give you a taster of what to expect. If you want to practise more, we would advise you to get an official practice test book. Remember to buy it *with* the audio as some books come without the audio. For additional practice you could also look at the audio scripts in the back of this book (pages 73–76), and explore them for distraction and paraphrasing.

Chapter 3
Speaking

The aim of each part

The Speaking test consists of three parts, and takes about 11–14 minutes. At the time of writing, the Speaking test is still done 'live', meaning you will be in a room with two other people (one who will ask you the questions, one who will be assessing your performance). You won't be with any other test takers.

In the first section of the test, you will be asked questions about yourself. These could be about your education, family, hometown, hobbies, likes/dislikes and so on. These questions are designed to help you feel at ease, and also to give you a chance to show how well you can answer relatively basic questions. Let's look at the kinds of questions that might come up:

1. What kinds of activities do you do in your spare time?
2. Tell me about your family.
3. Have you always lived in X?
4. What did you most enjoy studying at school?

There are certain kinds of language that you will probably find useful for this section. This includes using **verb combinations** (e.g. like/hate +ing), **comparatives** and **superlatives** (e.g. better, best, etc.), **tenses** (in the examples here you might need to use present simple, past simple and present perfect), and expressions of preference (e.g. I'd prefer), as well as vocabulary of topics about you such as family, hobbies, places and studying. If you're aiming for a high score, you should be using this kind of grammar accurately, and also some higher-level language if it's appropriate.

Higher-level language includes many components, but some examples of this language include **idiomatic expressions** (e.g. 'it runs in the family'), **inversion and emphatic structures** (e.g. 'What I particularly enjoy about hiking is being surrounded by nature') and **conditionals** (e.g. 'If I had more spare time, I'd quite like to take up tennis') among many more.

Part 1 is designed to be relatively easy. The questions and grammar focus on lower levels, and a B1 (pre-intermediate) candidate should be able to answer these questions without too much difficulty.

Part 2 is often considered the most difficult part of the test. This is because you have to speak alone for 1–2 minutes. You will have one minute to prepare for this before you need to speak. The examiner will give you a prompt card which will have a topic and points you will need to speak about. Here is an example of a prompt card:

> Describe a person who you admire a lot.
>
> You should say:
>
> - Who the person is
> - What they are like
> - How well you know them
>
> And explain why you admire them.

You have one minute to prepare your answer, so use the prompt well. Make sure that you answer all parts of the prompt. This will also give what you say structure, and enable you to say more. Like Part 1, Part 2 is still based on you, so you will not be asked to speak for an extended time on things that are in no way related to you. The examiner will probably ask you a few closing questions about what you talked about.

Exam Tip: Timing is probably one of the most important issues in Part 2, so before you do the test, practise speaking for 1–2 minutes on topics to give you an idea of time.

Part 3 is a discussion. The topics here will concern wider issues, so you will need to give your opinions on issues such as global warming, personality traits, education systems and so on. The topic is usually linked thematically to Part 2, so, for example, if we moved on from the Part 2 example question above, Part 3 questions could include:

1. Do you think celebrities are admired too much?
2. What kinds of people make good role models?
3. Can admiring a person be a negative thing?
4. Should children always respect their elders?

These questions have themes related to admiration and respect, but they are asking for your opinions about society and issues in general. This is something that, according to the

CEFR (Common European Framework of Reference), is a competence of individuals at level B2 (intermediate) and above, so essentially these questions are higher level and the language you need to use will also be higher level.

Part 3 requires you to show opinions, justify them, show degrees of certainty and show alternatives to real-world situations or future possibilities. It is important that you give full answers and reasons for your thinking. Try to hypothesise (put forward your opinion/ argument with reasoning). For example:

> *I think admiration can sometimes be negative. What I mean by this is that there are situations where people are admired for something which might not be a very positive quality. Take for example looking up to a celebrity simply for their looks. I'm not sure this kind of adulation really contributes anything positive to society.*

What are they looking for?

The IELTS Speaking test is marked on four criteria (areas): Fluency and Coherence, Lexical Resource, Grammatical Range and Accuracy, and Pronunciation. There is a public version of the descriptors for every level, so you can read much more about what each level requires for each part of the criteria. If you search on the internet for 'IELTS speaking public band descriptors', you should be able to see the version that is available to everybody. However, here is a quick explanation of what each criterion means:

Fluency and coherence

This is the ability to speak smoothly without long pauses, and to connect your speech well. A test taker who often pauses or hesitates, and who says small chunks of speech without connecting them with, for example, 'this is because …' or 'but I suppose, on the other hand …' is unlikely to do very well in this area.

Lexical resource

This is the amount and quality of vocabulary you can use. A lower-level test taker will only be able to use a small range of vocabulary on a topic, while a higher-level candidate should be able to use a wide range of vocabulary. So, it is worth thinking about synonyms and expressions you can use for each subject that might be discussed. Where possible, avoid too much repetition and try to vary your vocabulary.

Grammatical range and accuracy

This includes two parts: the amount of different structures you can use (Range) and how correctly you use them (Accuracy). If you are a first-language English speaker, you probably already use most of the structures without even recognising it. However, you would also be surprised by how many first-language speakers have long-standing errors in their grammar, so it might be worth checking your speech with someone who is a **language buff** (if you know anyone like that).

Pronunciation

Pronunciation can be a specific problem area for candidates from some countries. A lot of the focus in the public band descriptors is based on intelligibility (how well you can be understood). Your **intonation** (the rise and fall of speech) or word stress (the words you place importance on) are important in communicating what you want to say in English. Additionally, it may be worth doing a little research on common pronunciation problems in English in the area you are from. Common errors include, but are not limited to:

- distinguishing 'L' and 'R' sounds for many Asian countries
- distinguishing 'W' and 'V' sounds for many European countries
- distinguishing 'B' and 'V' sounds for Spanish speakers
- producing short 'I' sounds and regular past (–ed) endings for almost all speakers.

You should consider these four categories of the marking criteria when preparing for your IELTS Speaking test. Often, what can happen is that candidates can show fluency at the expense of accuracy or vice versa, but for a top band score, you really need to have fluency, accuracy, show a range of language and be easily understood.

Exam Tip: If you are a first-language English speaker, then you should have relatively little problem with fluency and pronunciation. Where you might have problems is not using a sufficient range of language to get the score you need. Try to reduce this problem by **hypothesising**, and imagining and explaining what things you would do differently or what things could be done differently. These types of explanations usually lead to higher-level language that will improve your score.

Make it interesting

Of course, you are not being examined on how interesting you are, but if you can say exactly what you want to say *and* you can use more interesting language to say it, you will do better. Let's look at an example of this:

Imagine two test takers are asked to tell the examiner about where they are from.

Candidate 1 I am from China. China is a very big country with a long history. China is a part of the Asian continent, and it is one of the biggest countries in the world and has many landscapes. I am from Fuzhou, which is a very big city in China.

Candidate 2 I am from China. It's a big country, actually about the size of the USA, and the climate changes dramatically, but, unlike the USA, we're just in one time zone. I am from one of the cities by the sea, Fuzhou. Perhaps it's not very well-known outside China, but it has over seven million people.

Hopefully, you think Candidate 2 is better, but let's think about what Candidate 1 said. What has the examiner found out about the candidate's home country? Nothing, except that they are from China. Most people know that China is a big country, and most countries have a long history. This is the kind of sentence that examiners might hear a lot, but it actually tells them nothing new, and makes the speaker seem like they have learned set phrases to an extent.

Candidate 2 has also said that China is a big country, but there is also more information. The candidate has given an interesting comparison, and possibly told the examiner something they didn't know before. We also have information about the city they live in. By expressing something more interesting, they've also used more interesting vocabulary (e.g. 'climate', 'dramatically', 'time zone'), which affects the score. This is true of every part of the Speaking test: Being interested and interesting will probably lead you to give better answers.

Let's look at the Part 3 question, and imagine two test takers giving their answers:

Examiner *What kinds of people make good role models?*

Candidate 1 I don't know. I think people who make a lot of money and have a lot of success make good role models. Maybe they make people work harder. For example, a businessman like Bill Gates or Steve Jobs. These are probably very positive role models because they both ran successful companies, and they both have a lot of money, and they are hardworking, and I think they both help other people. These are qualities that everyone should want.

Candidate 2 I'm not sure if there is any particular type of person that makes a good role model. I think people's role models are quite dependent on their situation and how they've been raised. In some contexts, a successful businesswoman could be a good role model for young girls, especially if they want to have more equality in their own lives, but that role model might not be so applicable for boys. People who have been brought up with a focus on morals, may aspire to people who work in charity. In a way, role models depend on what the individual aspires to, and there's not necessarily a formula.

Here, again, Candidate 2 is probably going to do better.

Candidate 1 doesn't have many ideas and repeats themselves. This test taker mentions twice that role models should make money, work hard and be successful, and this has also made the test taker repeat language (e.g. 'they both'). Their viewpoint is simplistic, and this often produces simplistic language. Probably the most complex use is 'both'.

However, Candidate 2 presents a more complex viewpoint. They are not sure that there is a 'kind' of good role model, and they explain why they think this by using **hypothetical** examples (e.g. 'a successful businesswoman could be ... if they want to have more equality ...'). The viewpoint here and the expression of this gives an impression of greater complexity compared to the more simplistic first answer.

Remember that although the examiner is trained to mark objectively, it is likely that they hear many candidates like 'Candidate 1', so try and stand out from the crowd.

Be 'creative'

Imagine that you go into the exam and you get a prompt asking you to describe the person you most admire. You've never thought about it before, and you're not really sure if you admire anyone. If this happens to you, don't spend valuable time assessing who the

Exam Tip: Hypothetical examples in Part 3 will produce higher-level language. Examples of this language include using **modal forms** (e.g. 'They could have ...' 'People might consider ...') or **passive modal forms** (e.g. 'Things could have been different ...') or **conditional forms** (e.g. 'If films and TV weren't so popular, we'd have fewer celebrity role models').

person you *really* admire the most is, just make something up! Pick a person, any person, and structure your speech around that. You do not need to tell the truth; this is not a test of your honesty.

This is especially important for younger candidates taking the test who may have little life experience, and therefore may find it difficult to answer questions about life experiences. Subjects such as 'the most exciting trip you've ever been on' can be quite intimidating, especially if you've never travelled further than 50km outside of your home town.

So, it's worth thinking of answers for questions that you really have no idea how to answer, and thinking of how you can make them interesting too. Let's explore the reasoning behind this with some more examples:

Examiner	*What's your favourite celebration?*
Candidate 1	*Silence* Errmmmm ... uhhhh ... hmmmm ... I'm not really sure ... Errmmmmm ... maybe Christmas ... hmmm but maybe New Year. I like that too.
Candidate 2	Well ... I think my favourite celebration is probably Holi, which happens here in India every spring. It's really amazing. If you haven't heard about it, it's where coloured powder is thrown ....
Examiner	*Tell me about your last holiday.*
Candidate 1	Err ... We don't have holidays ... We stay at home. Just see family.
Candidate 2	Ermmm ... well, we often stay at home and don't really go anywhere adventurous. But often during the holidays I stay at my grandparents' house and this is always exciting. Last time I helped my grandad on the farm.

Yet again, don't be Candidate 1. The examiner can't mark silence. Of course, you might need a bit of time, and there are some phrases which can give you more time, but don't overuse these. It's a speaking test, after all, so speak! Here are some phrases to give you a little more thinking time:

- *Let me think ...*
- *Well I'm not too sure, but ...*
- *I think if I had to choose one ...*
- *I've not really thought about that before, but ...*

Then, give your answer.

Keep going, you can do it! (and how)

Where possible, you should always try to give full answers. Short answers are terrible for the examiner and terrible for the test taker. Try to avoid this. Here is an example of a test taker giving short answers:

Examiner	*So, where are you from?*
Candidate 1	Rome.
Examiner	*What is Rome like?*
Candidate 1	Nice.

Think of it from the examiner's perspective: how can you assess that person's language? It's impossible. Even if the candidate gives full sentence answers to those questions, it doesn't show much more ability:

Examiner	*So, where are you from?*
Candidate 1	I'm from Rome.
Examiner	*What is Rome like?*
Candidate 1	It's nice.

Here, the candidate has produced sentences, but they're really basic. We could say this test taker is a beginner, but not much else. Of course, the questions are quite simple, and maybe the test taker will improve as they continue through the test, but the candidate could still do more with their answers to show they are higher level. Look at the following example:

Examiner	*So, where are you from?*
Candidate 1	I'm from Rome, actually just on the outskirts. I'm from a small place called Tor De Cenci, which is near a great nature reserve.
Examiner	*What is Rome like?*
Candidate 1	Well, it's obviously a very big city, and it's a great mix of modern and ancient architecture. I think it's a really beautiful place to live, but the traffic can be terrible.

Look at how much better that is. The way in which you can extend your answers can vary depending on the part of the test.

In Part 1, in which you are being asked about yourself, give details about your answers. For example, if the examiner asks you where you are from, give more information than just the place. You could say what it's famous for or say something about the geography of it. If they ask you about your favourite hobby, you could say why you like it or when you started doing it.

In Part 2, you definitely need to extend your answers because you need to speak for 1–2 minutes. Let's look at an example to see how you can do this:

> Describe a country you would like to visit.
>
> You should say:
> - Where it is
> - What special features it has
> - What you would like to see there
>
> And explain why you want to visit it.

So, let's imagine the country is Iceland. Here are some notes that a candidate could write before speaking to help them remember and organise these ideas:

Where: North Atlantic Ocean. Near Greenland. Quite isolated.

Special features: Lots of snow and ice. Some giant waterfalls. Unusual landscape. Maybe like being on the Moon!

See: Love to visit the capital Reykjavik. Go to the countryside. See geysers and waterfalls. Maybe go on a boat.

Why: Because I live in a hot country, and I would like to see something completely different.

Try speaking for 1–2 minutes with those notes (or you could make some notes of your own). Time yourself. Did you speak for long enough? If not, here are some suggestions of ways in which you could continue:

- Talk about your travel experiences in connection with Iceland: 'Actually, I've never been to a cold country on holiday. I've always had beach holidays in the past. Like the time I went to …'
- Talk about how you think Iceland is different from your home country: 'I imagine Iceland would be totally different to India, where I am from. It's a really …'
- Talk about how you found out about Iceland: 'I watched a travel programme …'; 'My best friend went there and told me …'

Now, if you didn't speak for long enough the first time, you could try again and use some of the suggestions above. Did you add more time to your speech?

In Part 3, you need to give your opinions, so a natural way of extending these is by giving reasons, talking about causes or consequences and imagining how things could be different. Let's look at how this could be done in answer to the question:

Do you think people should do more to prevent pollution?

- Giving reasons: 'I think people really need to think and do much more about pollution *because we've only got one planet and we shouldn't take it for granted.*'
- Talking about causes: 'I think we really should do much more about pollution. Not just individuals, but companies too, *as, in my opinion, large-scale production and shipping is what is causing most of the damage to our environment.*'
- Talking about consequences: 'We should absolutely do more to stop pollution. We only need to make small differences to our lives, but *if we carry on taking the planet for granted, it won't be a very nice place for future generations.*'
- Imagining how things could be different: 'I do think we should all try to do a bit more to prevent pollution. *Imagine if we went on unchecked using up all our natural resources and pumping pollutants into the environment. Our planet could end up looking like some kind of wasteland.*'

These are just some of the ways you can extend your speech, but remember, in a speaking test, you must speak. It's not a simple question-and-answer session. In order to show the examiner the range of language you can use, you should speak at some length when answering questions.

Think of your opinions

For some test takers, one of the most difficult parts of the Speaking test is Part 3, in which you need to give opinions on a topic. This can simply be because test takers don't really have an opinion on the topic or perhaps haven't thought about it before. The Speaking test is not the time to try to work out what you think about a certain subject. This would probably require too much thinking time, and therefore you might not speak enough.

There are two ways to deal with this: Firstly, you could quickly choose the first opinion you think of; secondly, you could think about your opinions on certain subjects before the test. The second option is probably wiser, as you might change your opinion as you speak if you just say the first thing that comes into your head.

Chapter 3 – Speaking

There are only so many subjects that can come up in the Speaking test, so brainstorm some typical discussion questions and think about your opinions on these topics. Topics can include: 'the environment', 'education', 'healthcare', 'media communications' and 'values'. This is not an exhaustive list, but if you have a look at the chapter subjects of most IELTS course books, you can see what kinds of topics are likely to appear. You could try to produce subject maps to help you think of possible issues within the area such as the following example

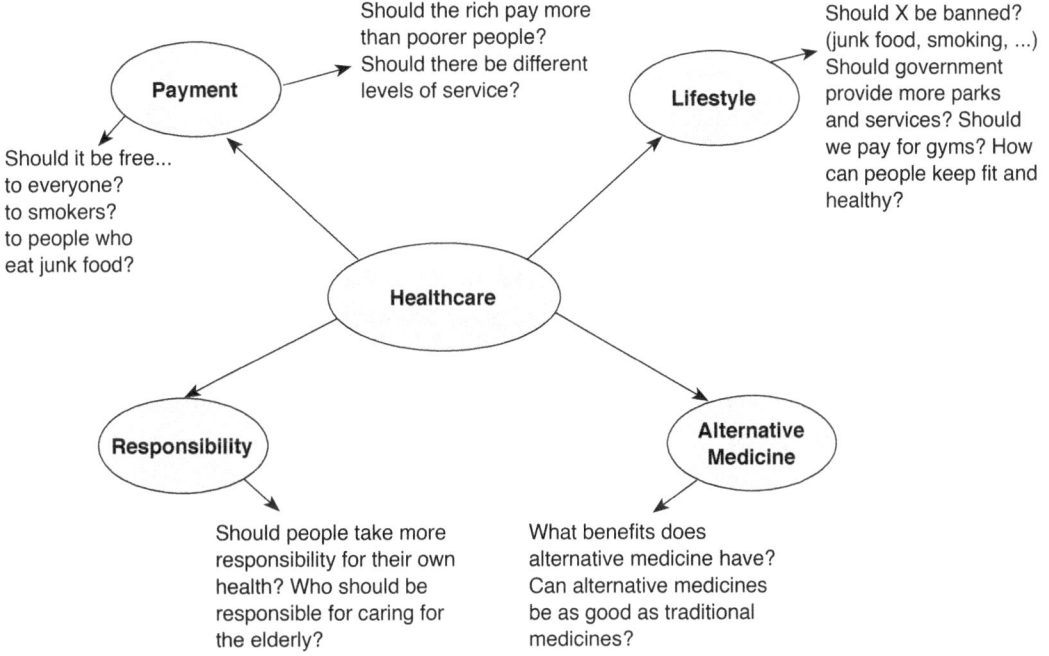

Exam Tip: These kinds of topics and questions overlap with Task 2 in the Writing test, so you can use these ideas for both writing and speaking.

Chapter 4
Reading

Time is tight

The Reading test can be one of the most difficult parts of the examination for many people, including first-language English speakers, and this is often due to the type of reading needed for the test.

There are three relatively long texts involved in the Reading test. These texts can be around 2,500 words in total (plus or minus 250 words), which is a lot to read. To give you an idea of how long that is, the introduction section in this book comprises around 1,750 words.

The problem with having texts of this length is that, within the hour, there is no time to carefully read every word and engage with the texts before tackling the questions. Each text will have a set of questions related to it (40 questions over the whole Reading test), and you have to answer these and transfer your answers to an answer sheet all within that time. This gives you 20 minutes per text to answer the questions and transfer these answers.

One of the most useful things you can do is practise your timing for this paper. You do not have to read all the text before answering the questions. Sometimes there are whole **paragraphs** with no questions related to them, so spending time reading and understanding those paragraphs is not necessary. Of course, you should find out what works for you, but we find it is much quicker to read the questions first and then look for the answers in the text. Many question types (which we shall look at later) are actually in the order of the text, so merely by looking at the questions you can understand the structure of the text.

Exam Tip: If a question seems particularly difficult, come back to it. And if you run out of time and have any selection questions left, pick any letter rather than nothing. Remember, you will definitely get no points for a blank answer, but if you write something, you might get it right (you do not lose points for getting anything wrong). You can also try to guess any leftover completion questions using words from the texts.

Chapter 4 – Reading

Because you can go back and forth within the text, reading is somewhat different from listening. You have the chance to read again, which you don't have in the Listening test, so in this chapter we'll be presenting and practising the question types as we move through, rather than in one final section.

Search first, read 'bits' later

One key to the Reading test is to know how to locate the answers to questions quickly. This is sometimes easy, and sometimes a little more difficult. Let's look at how this can be done, using just a few sentence completion questions (but you can do this with almost all the questions).

Set a timer for 20 seconds and look at the sample text on pages 77–78. Look briefly.
Do not read it all. You might want to look at the title and the first sentence of each paragraph. Let your eyes run over the text and let words jump out at you. You do not need to understand any of the text yet. Once the 20 seconds are finished, look at the following questions:

1. In the transit of Venus, the planet appears as a _____ against the <u>Sun</u>.
2. Le Gentil managed to plot a proportion of the _____ of <u>Madagascar</u> while away.
3. The second transit in <u>1769</u> was _____ by clouds.

You may be wondering why some of the words are underlined. This is because these are your search words. This underlining will not be done for you in the test; you must choose your own search words. These are probably the most unusual words in the sentence (also known as **low-frequency words**). For example, 'as' or 'away' are very common words that you'll probably come across a lot in the text, and are very likely to be written differently. You do not want to search for these! Unusual words are typically **nouns** (dates, names and places are especially useful for locating information). You should find either these words or similar or **synonymous** words in the text. Notice how 'Le Gentil', which you could consider quite an unusual couple of words, is not underlined. This is simply because the whole text is about Le Gentil, who is a man.

Try looking for the underlined (or similar) words in the text. Locate the areas, and this is where you are likely to find the answers. This approach can save you valuable time in the exam. Instead of leisurely reading and understanding all the text, search for the parts you need to read and then analyse these sections carefully.

That's the first part, the 'search'. Now, we're going to move onto the analysis: finding the right answer.

Paraphrasing is key

Let's go back to the questions in the previous section and think about them a bit more carefully. Don't go looking for the answer in the text until you are asked to. Here is the first question again:

1   In the transit of Venus, the planet appears as a _____ against the Sun.

Most of the text talks about the transit of Venus, so searching for 'Venus' might not be useful. We are looking for Venus appearing 'as a _____ against the Sun'. The word that you could most likely locate the answer is the word 'Sun'.

Now have a think of other ways that 'appears as' and 'against' could be written. You could note down your ideas.

Let's turn to the space. Usually, you should answer in three words or fewer (but do read the instructions). However, it's also really useful to know what kind of word(s) need to go in the space. By looking at the words around the space ('a _____ against the Sun'), we can see that we need a noun (the word 'a' needs to have a **noun** following it).

Now look at the appropriate section of text you've located, and try to find the answer.

Did you find it? Here you can answer the question in one, two *or* three words. The answer could be 'dot', 'black dot' or 'small black dot'. These are all acceptable answers because the two **adjectives** don't contain essential information for the answer, just extra information.

Also, look at how the question above is paraphrased: 'appears as' is paraphrased in the text as 'looks like', and 'against' is rephrased as 'moving across'.

Exam Tip: In completion questions, if the adjectives before a noun contain essential information to the meaning of the sentence, you must include them. If the adjectives can be discounted and the meaning is the same, you can choose to include them. But make sure you are *within* the maximum word number you can use.

Chapter 4 – Reading

Now try to do the second two questions on your own, and we'll then look at how they are **paraphrased**.

2   Le Gentil managed to plot some of the _____ of Madagascar while away.

Do you have your answer? Well, this one is easy to find because there's only one mention of Madagascar (where it says 'Madagascan' in Paragraph C). Again, we need a **noun**. To answer this, we just need to know that 'plot' is a synonym of 'mapped' (in the question frame, the past tense is given in the word 'managed'), and 'some' is 'a proportion'. The answer is 'coastline'.

3   The second transit in 1769 was _____ by clouds.

Dates are great. They are really easy to look for. This date appears three times, but the first time it's just an introductory mention. From our quick glance we can tell that the story is in **chronological** (time) order. Let's reduce the sentence down to 'the transit was _____ by clouds.' If you know your grammar, you'll know that we're probably looking for a **passive** construction. It's a reverse form of 'The clouds _____ the transit.', which would be the **active** sentence. So, we know that we're looking for a **past participle** at least, because that's how the passive is made. The answer is here in this sentence in the text: '… when the day of the second transit came around, the 4th of June 1769, the sky became overcast, and his view of the transit was obstructed.' To get this question right, you need to know that 'overcast' essentially means 'cloudy', and understand that 'his view was obstructed' is also essentially the same as 'the transit being obstructed'. You might think you can guess the answer without reading the text because common sense tells us that it's likely to be hidden or something similar, but you must use a word from the text. In this case '(completely) obstructed' is the answer. If you'd answered 'obscured' or 'hidden', or anything else for that matter, you would not get the mark.

Exam Tip: You must answer with a word or words from the text. Don't try to use your own knowledge or deduce the answer without using the passage.

The two question types

The question types for the Reading test are generally very similar to the listening question types, although there are some additional types in this section of the examination. As with the Listening test, your answers need to be spelt correctly, but we are not going to stress this quite as strongly here because, as opposed to the Listening test, you should

All About IELTS

be just copying. Any words you write as an answer to a completion question are just *copied* from the texts, so don't make a mistake with this! All questions will be testing your understanding of general ideas, specific information and direction of argument among other elements. Let's look at the question types you might get. We'll use examples from the reading text so you can see how the questions work.

Please note that, in the Reading test, you will see probably two or three question types and 13–14 questions for each text. For the purposes of introducing each question type, we have used the sample text with all the question types. This is not representative of the actual test.

Completion questions

With completion questions, you will normally see an instruction as follows:

Complete the X (sentences/flow chart/notes, etc.) below.

Write **NO MORE THAN TWO WORDS AND/OR A NUMBER** from the passage for each answer.

Exam Tip: Make sure you follow this word count. Hyphenated words are counted as one word. And if you write '$50', this is one word, while '50 dollars' is counted as two words. Every word is considered a word, so if you write for example 'a month', this is considered two words. You should always write within the word limit for each space. This is also true of listening completions.

Sentence completion

1   In the transit of Venus, the planet appears as a _____ against the Sun.

This was the example given earlier. Remember, try to identify the most unusual words in the question, and search for these or a **synonym** in the text. Then work out what kinds of words go in the space, and break down the parts of the question to find **paraphrases** in the text in order to locate the answer.

Chapter 4 – Reading

Summary completion

In our experience, summary completions generally **summarise** just a section of the text rather than the whole text, so look for the section that you think is summarised and focus on that. Here's an example:

> Le Gentil's first attempt to see the transit was filled with difficulties as the ship was diverted to Africa due to **1** _____. In addition to this, a **2** _____ had started in Pondicherry, and soon it became the jurisdiction of the **3** _____ As Le Gentil couldn't disembark here anymore he attempted to make his observations **4** _____.

This summary focuses on the second paragraph only to give you an example of what this question type looks like. You will probably find answers spread over two or three **paragraphs**. Essentially there is not too much difference between sentence and **summary** completions. You'll notice **paraphrases** in the summary and in the original text. The answers to this are: 'a monsoon', 'war', 'British' and 'at sea'. If you don't capitalise the 'B' in 'British' or use the 'at' in 'at sea', consider those answers incorrect.

Note completion

With note completions, you need to look at the grammar around the spaces to see how complete the grammar in the answers needs to be. This is similar to the listening in this respect.

> Le Gentil's trip
>
> **1** _____ – left France.
>
> 1761 – **2** _____ the first transit
>
> 1766 – decided to go to Manila

So, here we have a certain pattern in the response. We can work out that the first part requires a year, and that the second part requires a **verb** in the past (this is the pattern with 'left' and 'decided'). In this case, the answers are '1760' and 'missed'.

All About IELTS

Table completion

Tables aren't so different to note completions, so here is the very same question presented as a table, so you can see how they differ:

Le Gentil's trip	
Year	**Event**
_____	left France
1761	_____ the first transit
1766	decided to go to Manila

In fact, tables are often easier because they make it a bit clearer by how the information is organised. Here we can see that a year needs to go into the left-hand column, and voyage details in the right, because the table has headings. Similar to the note completion question, we know the information in the right-hand column doesn't need a subject (e.g. 'Le Gentil'/'he'), because none of the other information in that column has a subject. We just need to follow the format.

Flow-chart completion

A flow-chart completion is all about processes – what happens first, second, etc. Think of something simple such as sending a letter. You start by getting paper, writing the letter, putting it in an envelope, putting a stamp on it and then sending it. That's the process. The text doesn't really have many processes, but we can see an example, as the text is in chronological order, by looking at Le Gentil's journey:

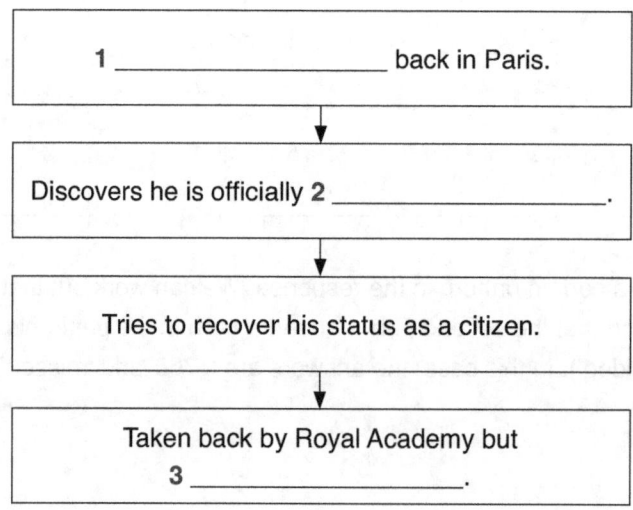

Here we can identify what types of words go in the spaces by looking at the words around them. If we look at the start of each sentence, we know that we need a verb for 1. And by looking at the context, and the word 'back', we can know that this is the end of the journey when he returns, and we can immediately go to the end of the text. The answer to 1 is 'arrived'. In the question it is 'arrived back in Paris', and in the text it is 'arrived home'.

For number 2, we are looking for an adjective (because 'officially' is an adverb which can describe an adjective, and we have the structure 'he is'). Here the answer is 'dead'. The answer is here in the text: 'he had been officially declared dead'. Here, 'officially' is synonymous with 'by the authorities'.

Lastly, we are looking for a negative point about being taken back (in the text 'reinstated') by the Royal Academy. The answer is in this part of the text: 'although in the end he achieved this, and was reinstated by the French Royal Academy, he was demoted for not obtaining the data that he set out to get'. The answer to 3 is 'demoted'.

Diagram label completion

This is visual labelling, which can consist of using words from the text or selecting from a list of information. For the sample text, there is a small process of how the transit works:

Timeline of the transit of Venus

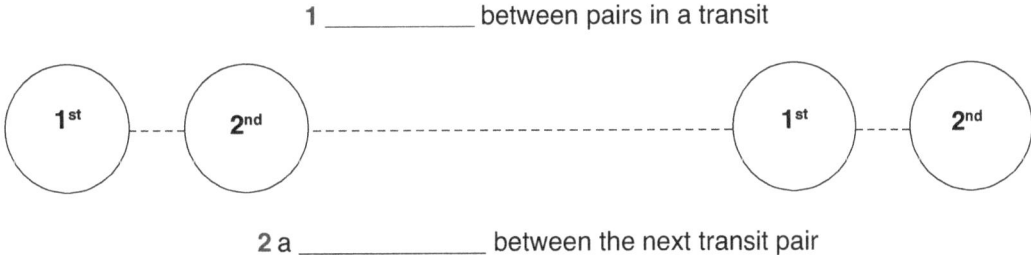

Here we can see a timeline of the transit. The important word here is 'timeline'. The diagram has no time periods, so we must need these at some point. The information here is in the first paragraph. The answer to number 1 is '8/eight years'. The answer is in this section: 'These transits come in pairs, which are usually eight years apart ...' The answer to number 2 is 'hundred years'. Remember that 'one' and 'a' have essentially the same meaning in this context. The answer is in this section: 'followed by long periods in between of over a hundred years.'

All About IELTS

Usually in the Reading test, the diagrams will not be as simple as this, but this gives a clear example showing how you need to understand the diagram and what information is needed before looking in the text. Look for clues such as dates and names, and try to work out how each part of the diagram relates to the other parts.

Short answer questions

These kinds of questions just require a few words for the answer, not a full sentence. Here's an example:

> How long did his entire voyage take?
> The answer is '11 years'.

Selection questions

This question type comprises the following variations.

Multiple choice

Again, these are very similar to those in the Listening test, but here there are four options to choose from, and you must select the one right answer.

> Le Gentil observed and recorded features of …
> A   Manila
> B   Madagascar
> C   Île de France
> D   Pondicherry

Here the answer is *B* because he 'mapped' Madagascar, which has a similar meaning to 'observe' and 'record'. 'Observe' is also **distracting**, as in the text it is used with other places to describe his viewing of the transit of Venus.

Exam Tip: A lot of the advice for selection questions in the Listening section is also true here. You can use many of the same techniques.

Chapter 4 – Reading

Identifying information (True/False/Not Given)

In these questions, you'll see a sentence, and you have to decide whether the information in the sentence is true or false according to the text, or whether we cannot know if it's true or false (not given). Here is a sample with the instruction:

Do the following statements agree with the information in the passage?

Write

TRUE if the statement agrees with the information

FALSE if the statement contradicts the information

NOT GIVEN if there is no information on this

1 When Le Gentil arrived back in Paris, he was fired from the academy.

Before reading on, look at the text and decide what you think the answer might be. 'Not given' answers are especially hard to find because the answers are not in the text. With True/False/Not given questions (as with Yes/No/Not given questions described later on), we need to check that all parts of the sentence agree, or whether any directly disagree in the text. The answer to the question above is *False*. He had lost his job, but because they thought he was dead, they did not fire him.

Look at the following three sentences. Which is true? Which is false? Which is not given? Why?

A Le Gentil's data from the first transit were largely imprecise.
B Le Gentil's data from the first transit were incomplete.
C Le Gentil's data from the first transit were exact.

Firstly, yes, data is **plural** and goes with a plural verb ('were', not 'was'). The answer to the sentences above is in the following sentence:

While he managed some measurements while at sea, these were largely useless, as the movement of the ship greatly affected the accuracy of the measurements.

The first sentence (A) is *True* because 'imprecise' has the same meaning as 'inaccurate'. The second sentence (B) is *Not given*, because there is no mention in the text about how complete the data were, only how accurate they were. The third sentence (C) is *False* because 'exact' is the opposite of 'inaccurate'.

Now let's change another part of the sentence:

> Le Gentil's data from the second transit were largely imprecise.

Look again at the text. Would you say this sentence is true, false, or not given? In fact, the answer would not be *Not given*, because we know that his view was obstructed, but the text doesn't mention whether he managed to get any data or not on the 'second transit'.

Another problem is that some candidates take a very long time to answer 'Not given' questions. This is because they are looking for information that just simply is not there, so if you can't find one part of the sentence in the text, don't wait too long and choose *Not given*.

Identifying a writer's views/claims (Yes/No/Not Given)

These are similar to True/False/Not given questions, but here you are asked to check whether the statements agree with a person's view (for example, the writer or a person in the text). Here is an example:

> The writer believes that Le Gentil was unfortunate.

We have to be careful to check that the text shows the writer's opinion. In the text, we can see that the writer uses the word 'tragedy' (last paragraph), which indicates he/she thinks Le Gentil was unfortunate, so we can say this is *True*. Even the text title questions whether he was the 'unluckiest' astronomer in the world. If there were no words to give this opinion, we would have to answer Not given, even if our opinion, based on the text, is that he is unlucky.

Matching questions

We've put three types of matching questions together because they are very similar and use similar techniques. For some matching questions, the paragraphs in the text will be lettered (e.g. A–E). The first paragraph is A, the second B, and so on.

For **information matching**, you need to read the sentences and match them to where in the text you will find them, and when **matching features** you will have a list of items (perhaps names, places and/or dates) and you need to match them to the information in the sentences by reading the passage. You may also need to **match sentence endings**.

In these question types you will see a number of sentence beginnings and sentence endings, which you will need to put together using your knowledge from the text.

Here is an example of each:

Information matching: Which paragraph **A–E**:

1. Says that Le Gentil was under suspicion by a country?
2. Shows the purpose of monitoring the transits?
3. Gives a successful activity that Le Gentil undertook?

Here, you need to identify where the information is and write down the corresponding paragraph letter. You can tackle these questions in any order you want. Firstly, underline the key words in the questions, think of any synonyms, and look for this information in the text. So, for example in Sentence 1, you would underline 'suspicion' and 'country' ('Le Gentil' is throughout the text). In Sentence 2, 'purpose' and 'transits', and so on. The answers to this question are: 1 C; 2 A; 3 C.

Feature matching: Match the places (**1–3**) with the descriptions (**A–C**).

1	Pondicherry	A	where Le Gentil was rerouted
2	Manila	B	where Le Gentil was under suspicion
3	Île de France	C	where nations fought over

In this question type, the text will not be labelled with A, B, C, etc. With feature matching, tackle these questions in the order that you are most sure of. So, if you think you know the answer to 3, answer this first (but make sure you write your answer in the correct space on the answer sheet). This is because if you do these in order, you may use an option which is actually correct for a later question. It is a good idea to find the feature (in this case the country) and then read around where it is mentioned in the text in order to find the answer. The answers to this question are: 1 B; 2 A; 3 C.

Sentence ending matching: Match the sentences (**1–3**) with their endings (**A–C**).

1	Le Gentil was one of many astronomers who were …	A	reinstated in the Royal Academy.
2	Le Gentil had to work hard upon his return to France to be …	B	tasked with measuring both transits.
3	Le Gentil would have seen if the second transit if Manila had …	C	allowed him to remain.

All About IELTS

You will need to read the text in order to answer these, and also use the grammatical clues in the sentence halves. Look at option C above. We can see the word 'him' in this half of the sentence, so we know that the first half cannot be 1, because the subject is **plural** ('many astronomers'). Grammatically, you might be able to discount some options, which will make it easier to find the answers, but not all options. You will still need to check against the text. You may also have extra options which you will need to discount.

Matching headings

Matching headings questions are a little different from the other matching questions because you need to have a general understanding of the theme of each paragraph, and be able to identify the correct heading for this theme. Often, it is advisable to just look at the first sentence of a paragraph to identify the theme, but this can lead to errors in this question type (sometimes the first sentence can just be a transitional sentence that leads from the topic before to the next topic, and so on). It is best to try to work out what the key subject of the paragraph is by looking at the more **low-frequency words** within it, and then think about their connection. Also, it can be very useful to discount the options that you know are definitely wrong before deciding on the right one.

In fact, when matching headings, it is sometimes more useful to tackle these questions by focusing on the headings and paragraphs you are most sure of first, and work through them until you're left with the ones you are least sure of. If you work through the text from paragraphs A to E it may be more difficult and time-consuming to match the headings if you are not sure, and you may discount an answer that was right for another heading.

Let's look at an exemplar heading matching question, using the reading text on pages 77–78.

> The reading text has five sections A–E. Choose the correct heading for sections **B–E** from the list of headings below. Write the correct number **i–vi** in the boxes. There is one more heading than you need.
>
> i   *A natural 'disaster'*   EXAMPLE: A = v
> ii *Issues from territorial disputes*
> iii *Proving his status*
> iv *Frustration with governments*
> v   *A rare sighting*
> vi *A new site lost*

Essentially, you need to look at the list of headings above and decide which paragraphs they go with. You should write the Roman numeral (e.g. 'iv') as your answer, not the heading title. You can try to match all the headings now if you want to, but let's take a look at Paragraph C and try to match it with a heading.

> This did not deter Le Gentil, as he decided to wait the eight years necessary for the next transit to be seen, without returning to France. In these years between transits, Le Gentil mapped some of the Madagascan coastline. By 1766 he decided that Manila could make a perfect observation point for this next transit. Having written to request official papers from the French Royal Academy, who had originally commissioned his voyage, he set sail again, this time for Manila. When he reached Manila and received word from the Academy that he could have diplomatic papers for his study, amazingly, authorities in Manila couldn't believe the speed at which a response came from the Academy, and he was accused of being a spy and had to return to his original plan, heading once more to Pondicherry, which had been restored into French governance.

The more **low-frequency words** have been underlined in this paragraph. We can immediately discount two headings as there is no mention of natural disasters (i) or territorial disputes (ii). There are some possible options that seem to jump out of this text: Proving his status; Frustration with governments; A new site lost.

Let's look at these in turn.

You may think *Proving his status* (iii) is correct, as he asked for the Royal Academy to send papers, but this is only a sentence or two in the paragraph, and also the papers in the end didn't prove his status, so we must discount this.

Let's consider *Frustration with governments* (iv). We can see the government didn't believe he was an astronomer. They thought he was a spy, so he couldn't stay. However, this is just mentioned at the end of the paragraph, and the paragraph doesn't state whether he was frustrated or not, so we must discount this.

The answer is therefore *A new site lost* (vi). This covers more of the paragraph. The new site is Manila, and he couldn't stay there because of the government.

Here is the rest of the key: B = ii; C = vi; D = i; E = iii

All About IELTS

Completing your answer sheet

Remember that unlike the Listening test, in which you have transferal time for your answers, in the Reading test, you need to make sure that you have your answers written on the answer sheet within the allocated 60 minutes. There is no extra time.

The answer sheet has 40 numbered spaces for your answers. Take time to copy your answers accurately, and make sure that you put the correct answer next to the correct number. Remember, if it is inaccurate in any way, the answer will be marked as incorrect.

Exam Tip: If you have any time left in the test, go back and make sure that you have spelt words correctly from the text, and that all instructions have been followed (e.g. format of answer and number of words).

Chapter 5
Writing

Task 1: Visual information

There are two tasks in the Writing test. In Task 1, you will see some visual information. This could be presented in several forms, such as a graph, chart, map or diagram. You will then need to **summarise** the information by selecting and writing about the **main features**, and making comparisons of the data if there are any comparisons that can be made. This is the smaller of the two tasks. It requires the fewest words (you should write at least 150 words), and it is worth fewer marks than Task 2, so spend less time on this section accordingly. The recommended time to spend on this is 20 minutes.

Exam Tip: You don't have to do the tasks in any particular order, so it is worth starting with the higher-value task, the essay, if possible. Give yourself 40 minutes for the essay, and 20 minutes for the visual information.

In this section, we're going to focus on an example of visual data in the form of a bar chart. This will focus on wider advice that you should remember for Task 1, but we will also present you with examples and sample answers for other types of Task 1 visuals that you might get so you can see an example of answers for different kinds of information.

Exam Tip: In our experience, you're probably more likely to get a chart or a graph of some kind than anything else, but there is always a chance that you might get something out of the ordinary, so practise describing a range of visuals before the test.

Here is a sample task. You will see the visual data and an instruction similar to this:

> The following graphs give information about types of online activities separated by gender for the years 2011 and 2016. Summarise the information by selecting and reporting main features, and making comparisons where appropriate.

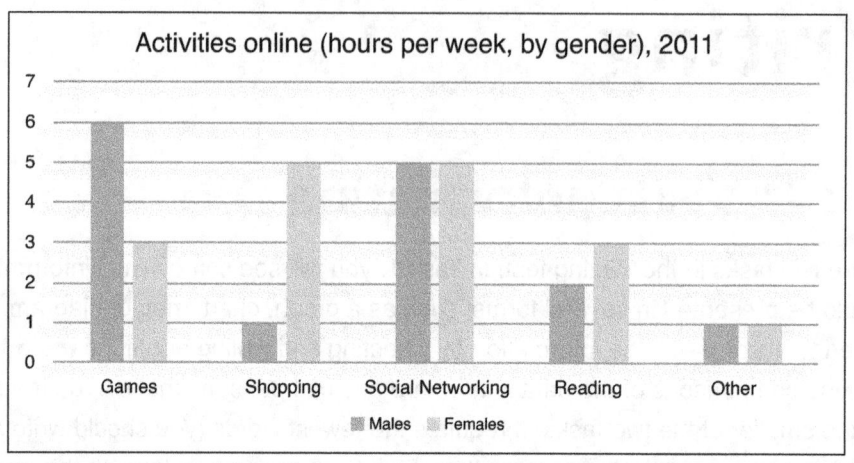

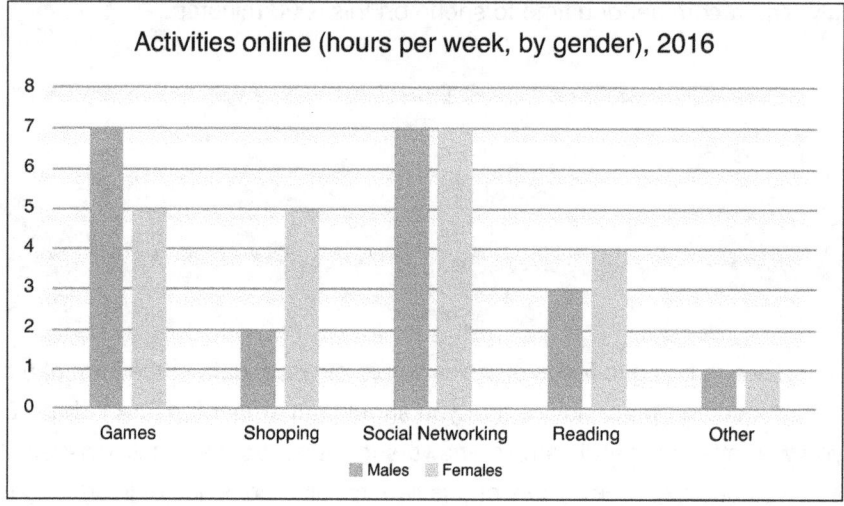

Before you continue reading the rest of this chapter, try to write an answer for this sample task. Remember, you need <u>at least</u> 150 words, but try not to write more than 250 words, and time yourself 20 minutes for the task. Then go back to your writing after reading each of the following sections, and assess it with this advice in mind. Would you change anything?

Exam Tip: The Writing test states only a minimum number of words to write. Make sure that you write more than the minimum. However, don't write substantially over the word count (by, for example, hundreds of words), because your writing may decrease in quality. Remember, it is about quality rather than quantity.

What are they looking for?

Task 1 of the IELTS Writing paper is marked under the following four categories: Task Achievement; Coherence and Cohesion; Lexical Resource; and Grammatical Range and Accuracy. There is a public version of these marking criteria, and you can find it by searching online using the term 'IELTS Writing Task 1 public band descriptors'.

Let's look at each of these and what they mean:

Task Achievement

This basically means 'have you done what you were asked to do?' So, for Task 1: have you summarised the information, identified and reported the key trends/features and, if possible, made comparisons with the information you have?

Coherence and Cohesion

This refers to how you have ordered your information (is it clear and logical?) and whether you have paragraphed clearly. It also is about how well your sentences connect. There are two main aspects of connecting information: firstly, having a logical structure; and secondly, using words such as 'so', 'but' and phrases that link to information given in the sentence before (e.g. 'this increased later in the decade…'; 'the figures started to fluctuate after this'). These phrases and words **connect** the pieces of information.

Lexical Resource

This refers to the use of vocabulary. Where possible, try to paraphrase words or phrases from the graphs. This can't always be done as some words in Task 1 are very specific, but if you can, do it! Also think about the vocabulary you need to accurately talk about this kind of information (generally this is data language such as 'significant increase', 'general decline', 'stable', etc.).

Grammatical Range and Accuracy

This is about how many grammatical structures you use, and how accurately you use them. One tip for Task 1, especially if you have a graph, is to ensure that you understand what time the graph is focused on (e.g. past, present or future, or a mixture). This will tell you what tenses you need to use in your writing.

Keep all of these criteria in mind when you are practising your writing as they are all equally important in gaining a good score. You can remember them more easily by thinking of this acronym:

F – flow (connecting your ideas and structuring your work)
L – lexis (using a variety of appropriate words)
A – answer (following the instructions and answering the question)
G – grammar (accurately using the correct grammar needed in the task)

Give it some meaning

You must explain what the graphs mean. This may seem a strange thing to read, but you would be surprised by how many people describe each element of the graph without actually explaining what the information is communicating.

Firstly, let's explore what these kinds of graphs are about. When are graphs used and why? Often, graphs are used to communicate relatively complex data quickly. Imagine this scenario: you're a super successful businessperson, and you have very little time to spare to analyse data yourself. You pay people to do that for you, giving you the 'big picture' so you can make a decision. Which of the following employees would you prefer to hear from?

Employee 1	Well, in 2010 the sales of our products were quite steady, and we sold about 6,000 units to China, 2,000 units to Japan, and 3,000 units to other Asian countries. We sold 7,500 to Canada and the USA. We didn't sell anything in South America or Africa. We had sales of around 1,000 to 2,000 in most European countries. In total that's about 20,000 units. In 2016, we had around 10,000 sales in Europe overall. We sold 8,000 to Canada and the USA, and we sold 7,000 to China, 5,000 to Japan, and 5,000 to other Asian countries. There were no sales in South America, but sales of 500 in Africa.
Employee 2	Our sales base is changing geographically. When we compare the 2010 and 2016 figures, although we used to sell the most in Europe, this has decreased significantly. In fact, it has halved, while in Asia and Northern America sales are growing. We're also achieving a small number of sales in Africa, which is a new market for us.

Hopefully, you see the value of what the second employee says here, because they aren't just listing the figures; they are explaining what those numbers mean. When writing about data, be Employee 2 and think about what the graphs are trying to communicate.

Chapter 5 – Writing

Overview means overview

When you are writing about the information of a graph, you will need to begin with an overview. In our view, it's best to put this information at the beginning of your writing, although there is no firm rule on this. Our reasoning behind this is that, to signpost what you are talking about and what the information means, it is clearer to summarise at the start.

Your opening paragraph should do two things: 1) explain what the information is about, and 2) summarise the key message the information gives. Remember, a summary doesn't focus on the details – it gives the big picture. Look at these two introductory paragraphs (based on the chart at the start of this chapter). Which one do you think is better and why?

> The charts show the kinds of activities that people spend time on when on the internet. They offer a picture of differences in time spent by gender, and also over two time periods. Generally, the time people spent on the internet increased, while there are only marked differences in activities between men and women in two areas: gaming and shopping.

> The charts show the kinds of activities that people spend time on when on the internet. They offer a picture of difference in time spent by gender, and also over the two time periods of 2010 and 2016. Gaming was most popular for men, and shopping was more popular for women by around three to four hours. Both men and women spent time social networking, and this grew by two hours a week over 2010 to 2016. Not much time was spent on other activities.

Hopefully, you think the first paragraph is better. The main area in which these two introductory paragraphs differ is in the provision of an overall picture (Paragraph 1), while the second paragraph lists what happens in most categories. Also, we can see that the second paragraph has given us some detail (e.g. 'by two hours'; 'three to four hours'), which is probably best used in the main paragraphs. It would be fine to mention the years in the opening paragraph, but think carefully about giving any more detailed figures or listing categories.

Groups and trends

When writing the **main body** paragraph(s), do not just move from one piece of data to another, describing them in turn. Listing categories and perhaps simple changes that occur within them doesn't particularly '**summarise**' but rather '**describes**'. These words are different! Descriptions are generally something lower-level candidates can do.

You need to work with the information. You need to think of ways you can group the data. This will also make comparisons easier to do. For the graphs presented here, one of the clearest ways to group the information could be through the following points:

- The differences between men and women over time
- The growing similarities between men and women over time
- Stability between men and women over time
- Overall trends in internet use

This also gives you some kind of structure to work with. When you look at these four bullet points, you can also get a sense of how to logically separate paragraphs. Remember, it's only 150 words, so you probably won't write more than three paragraphs in total. A sample structure could be as follows:

- Introduction – Summary of what graph is about and the main trends
- Main body 1 – Differences, similarities, and stability differences in data
  (or Main body 1 – Differences; Main body 2 – Similarities and stability)
- Conclusion – A short (1–2 sentence) summary of overall trends

Representing the facts clearly

In your main body, after grouping and explaining the data, you will need to give some facts and figures relating to the information. Think of this as evidence to support your trend identification.

When describing the trends, and supporting these trends with data, accuracy of language is especially important. You need to be very clear about the data and express them accurately. There are a number of considerations when doing this. Firstly, think about the time(s) so that you know which tense(s) to use. Make sure that you think about this before you start writing. If you aren't used to the terms of grammar here, don't worry too much because it is likely that you use the different tenses already but just don't know their names. These two graphs are from 2011 and 2016, so everything you use should be in some form of the past tense. Because we are talking here about doing activities in the past, there will be a lot of past continuous and past simple:

> Males were spending most of their time online playing games in 2011.
> In 2011, shopping and social networking were the most popular ways of spending time on the internet for females.

When referring to the change between two graphs, the past simple can be used again, or you can use the past perfect:

> The time women spent gaming grew between 2011 and 2016.
> The amount of time spent on social media had risen by 2016.

The second thing you need to make sure you do is use **prepositions** well (e.g. 'at', 'by', 'from' and 'to'). Look at how a mistake with prepositions can change the entire meaning of your sentence:

> Time spent social networking grew *by* two hours per week for both males and females.
> Time spent social networking grew *from* two hours per week for both males and females.
> Time spent social networking grew *to* two hours per week for both males and females.

Here, the first sentence is correct, and the other two sentences completely misrepresent the data.

You can show how the data change in other ways, for example: using fractions or percentages. So, if men spent on average two hours a week reading in 2011 and this rose to three hours in 2016, we could also say 'the time men spent on reading rose by 50%', or 'the time men spent reading rose by a half'. If you're not confident with numbers, don't worry about this too much. Remember, it's an English test, not a maths test. It is useful because it gives you an opportunity to express the changes in different ways.

Sample answer

Here is a sample answer. There are many ways in which you can write a great answer, and it is quite possible to focus on different **main features**. However, you could use this answer as an example of good practice for the test. If you try to follow the advice above, and your English is already very good, you are likely to do well in this part of the test.

> The graphs below give information about types of online activities separated by gender for the years 2011 and 2016. Summarise the information by selecting and reporting main features, and making comparisons where appropriate.

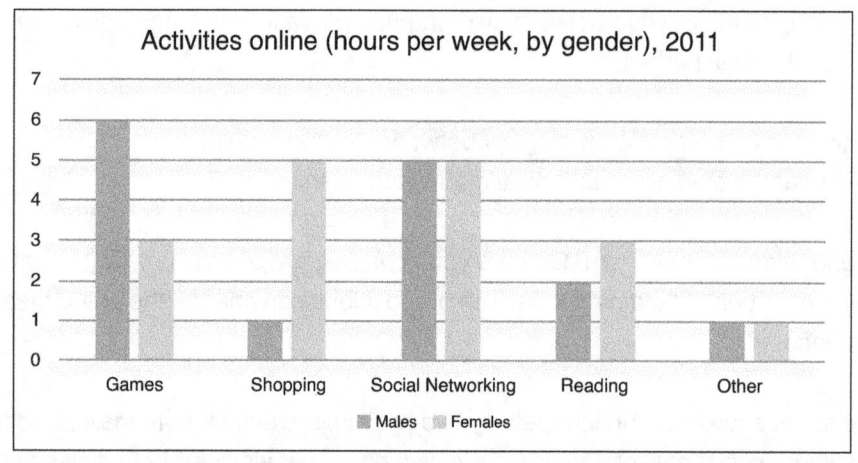

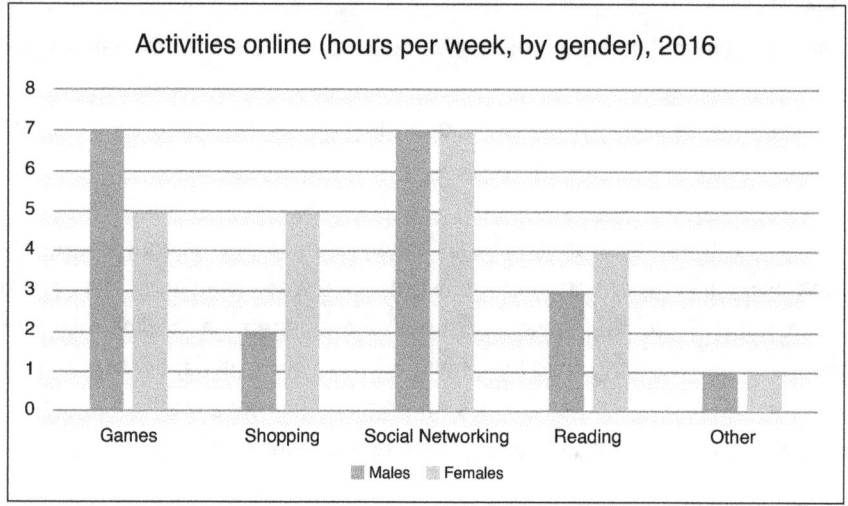

The charts show the kinds of activities that people spend time on when on the internet. They offer a picture of differences in time spent by gender and also over two time periods. Generally, the time people spent on the internet increased, while there are only marked differences in activities between men and women in two areas: gaming and shopping.

In both years, women spent more time on shopping, while men spent more time gaming. In 2011 and 2016, respectively, men spent six hours and seven hours on gaming, in comparison to women (three hours and five hours per week). Women spent five hours on shopping online (both in 2011 and 2016), while men only spent a few hours on this.

Generally, the areas of social networking and reading were very much a shared domain for both men and women. Both in 2011 and 2016, males and females spent a comparable amount of time on social networking (five and seven hours, respectively), while reading and other activities seem to also have a relatively even distribution. Overall, differences between men and women lessened during these years, and social networking grew in popularity.

(191 words)

This section has focused on a bar chart, however the advice given does not vary widely for the other types of visual information. Please see pages 79–83 for other types of visual information and sample answers.

Task 2: Essay

For the second task in the Writing test, you need to answer an essay question. This is worth more marks than Task 1, and you need to write more (at least 250 words), so you should spend about 40 minutes on this task.

The essay task is usually in the form of a statement followed by an instruction asking you for your opinion on the statement. Here is an example:

> Schools should not just teach traditional subjects like maths and language. It is also their responsibility to address the wider demands and responsibilities involved in being a productive and positive part of society.
>
> To what extent do you agree or disagree with this statement?
>
> Give reasons for your answer and include examples from your own knowledge or experience.

Before you do anything, it is essential that you break the question down and understand all the parts to the statement. Rewriting the statement can help you do this. In the title above there is one key part:

Is it a school's responsibility to also teach young people how to contribute to society?

As with Task 1, you can try to write your essay to this question now. Write more than 250 words (but try not to write more than 350 words), and, if possible, time yourself. Then, when you read the advice in the following sections, go back and look at your writing. Would you change anything?

What are they looking for?

Task 2 of the IELTS Writing test is marked under the following four categories: Task Achievement, Coherence and Cohesion, Lexical Resource and Grammatical Range and Accuracy. There is a public version of these marking criteria, and you can find it by searching online using the term 'IELTS Writing Task 2 public band descriptors'. As you can see, the parts are the same as in the Task 1 marking criteria, so we won't give a general description of what they mean again. Let's focus on the *differences* between Task 1 and Task 2 instead:

Task Achievement

Again, this basically means 'have you done what you were asked to do?', but in this case, it is more about argument development. Here you need to provide your position (opinion) clearly, and develop an argument explaining why you think this. This means creating main points and providing supporting evidence or argument for them.

Coherence and Cohesion

This is very similar to Task 1. Your paragraphing needs to be very clear. Apart from the introduction and conclusion, each paragraph should present an overall point, which you then go on to explain and develop in that paragraph. It is also about how well your sentences connect. There are two main ways of connecting information: firstly, having a logical structure; and secondly, using words such as 'so', 'but' and phrases such as 'This in turn might affect…'; and 'A further argument against…'. These phrases and words connect the last piece of information to the next piece of information.

Lexical Resource

This means your use of vocabulary. Where possible, try to paraphrase words or phrases from the question. Try to vary your vocabulary and be precise in terms of what you mean. So, for example, when writing about being 'a part of society', you could use 'member of society', 'citizen' or 'member of the community'.

Grammatical Range and Accuracy

This is about how many grammatical structures you use, and how accurately you use them. One tip for Task 2 is that, when developing an argument, you may need a lot of modal verbs (e.g. 'should,' 'could,' and 'must'), as well as conditional structures (e.g.

'If students learn more social skills, it could result in a more peaceful society'), so if you haven't practised this for a while, it's worth revisiting these kinds of structures.

Developing your ideas

The first thing you need to be able to answer the essay question is ideas, and then an opinion. Depending on your age and background, this can either come easily for you, or you might find this difficult. You also need the ability to organise your ideas, and think about what your main points are and how you can develop them. Also, consider any smaller points and whether they belong as a supporting point to a main point or whether they are separate.

If you have problems thinking of ideas, start by reading around the subjects you might get asked about. The subject areas are not limitless, and you can see a list of these as the chapter topics of most IELTS books. They include areas such as health, education, the environment, crime, technology, the media and personality. Make a list of topics and their sub-topics, and start mapping out opinions and ideas. Here is an example:

CRIME AND PUNISHMENT

- Prisons: Are they a good thing? Are they effective? Are they too expensive?
- Rehabilitation: Do people deserve it? Does it work?
- Criminals: Why do people commit crimes? Are there different reasons?
- Crime: Are all crimes the same? Does anything ever make a crime acceptable?
- Technology: How have online crimes affected us? Should we be able to download films/music for free?

You could also create a subject map of ideas, as suggested in the Speaking chapter of this book. With all of these sub-topics and questions, think of your overall answer. Then, it is important to ask yourself *why* you have the opinions you have. This gives you reasons for your opinions. Looking at topics in this way and researching your ideas can also improve your vocabulary.

A good essay is an organised essay

Organising your answer in your essay is essential. You need an essay plan for your arguments and reasons. If you write new thoughts as they come into your head, your essay will be disorganised, and you are likely to lose marks on coherence and cohesion and possibly task achievement.

There are many ways to organise your essay points. In this example, we'll use a table:

> *Schools should not just teach traditional subjects like maths and language. It is also their responsibility to address the wider demands and responsibilities involved in being a productive and positive part of society.*
>
> *To what extent do you agree or disagree with this statement?*
>
> *Give reasons for your answer and include examples from your own knowledge or experience.*
>
> **Overall opinion: AGREE**

MAIN 1:	MAIN 2:	MAIN 3:
Understanding social responsibilities important	**Too much focus on academic areas**	**Too much power of schools if they teach social elements**
WHY?	**WHY?**	**WHY?**
• cultivates community ideas • helps students think of bigger issues • better in schools as parents may have varying ideas	• students who don't do well feel bad • too much stress on students	• possible indoctrination • how are these standards set?

Here we can see that main points have a theme, and then the bullet points that follow explain these themes a bit more. This is key to organising your own ideas for your essay. These main points will make the paragraphs, and the bullet points will be included (expanded upon) within each paragraph. Take some time to look at this table, and notice how the main points are wider arguments while the bullet points are more specific developments or explanations of these arguments.

Exam Tip: You can draw a grid or table quickly to note your main points and supporting points. It does not have to take too long. Remember that writing an essay is a process. You may decide to leave one main point out as you have a sufficient argument without it, or you may choose to reorganise ideas.

Notice that the third main point is a **counter argument**. This means that it gives the opposite side from what our main opinion is. It is a good idea to have one counter argument in your essay because it shows more balance. In other words, you need to show that you can see another point of view. If you add a counter argument, just remember that you need to explain why your main argument is still stronger. For example:

Even though there is a chance that this could give schools too much power, if citizenship studies were carefully planned by varying community groups this could lessen that power and provide a valuable learning experience.

Let's look at an action plan for organising your essay answer:

1. Write down your ideas relating to the question given.
2. Group ideas into main themes or arguments.
3. Put explanations or examples below each corresponding main theme.
4. Decide which points are stronger to give you your overall 'for or against' answer.
5. Think about a counter argument. Do you have any points to include on the opposite side? Why are they not so strong?
6. Decide the order in which your main themes or arguments will be presented.

This will give you a plan of what will go in your **main body** paragraphs. The only thing you need to think of now is the **introduction** (the first paragraph) and **conclusion** (the last paragraph). Your essay must include both of these, and they do similar jobs: the introduction should have some general information about the theme of the essay, and then the answer to the question; the conclusion should summarise the key points of the essay, and then restate your answer.

Exam Tip: A common way of describing an essay is as a burger. The bun is bread, and it tells you what it is. There is bread on the top (introduction), and the same type of bread is on the bottom (the conclusion). These parts are similar and don't include anything too detailed. In the middle goes the meat (the main body), which is full of argument and support. This is a useful way of thinking about an IELTS essay.

An English essay answers and never deviates

It is essential to remember that you are not just generally writing about the subject – there is a question in the title for you to answer, and you must answer it. Let's look at the example question again:

> Schools should not just teach traditional subjects like maths and language. It is also their responsibility to address the wider demands and responsibilities involved in being a productive and positive part of society.
>
> To what extent do you agree or disagree with this statement?
>
> Give reasons for your answer and include examples from your own knowledge or experience.

Here, the question is whether you agree or disagree with the opinion given. You need to state your answer to this question in your introduction and then write about why you think that in your main paragraphs and conclusion. You should *not* be writing about the positives and negatives of learning traditional subjects. This is not the question. You should be writing about whether schools should also teach how to be a part of society.

If you just write about the topic without addressing the question specifically, you will lose marks on task achievement, so make sure that you identify what the question is asking you, and focus on that for the whole essay. In some cultures, it is quite common to **deviate** and discuss things only loosely related to the subject, and in some cultures it is normal to leave your answer to the end. However, for many English language cultures, you must give your answer at the start and not deviate. Follow three easy rules for your whole essay:

1. State your answer in the opening paragraph.
2. Focus your main paragraphs on explaining why that is your answer.
3. Summarise and restate your position.

Include in your opening paragraph a sentence that clearly answers the question. For example:

> *I believe that schools should include social responsibility education in their curricula.*

Exam Tip: Try not to use 'I' in your essay other than in the sentence that states your opinion.

Don't be too strong

When writing an essay in English, it is also important to be careful with the language you use. Look at the following examples:

Teaching citizenship in schools will make society a better place in which to live.
Teaching citizenship in schools could make society a better place in which to live.

Using 'will' in the first sentence is a very definite answer, and we do not know that it will *definitely* lead to a better society. If it is likely, but not definite, think of using words such as 'might' or 'could'. This is because we are discussing a theoretical future that we cannot predict with certainty.

We can also distance ourselves somewhat from our opinion, and therefore make our essay seem a little more objective. You might have heard that using 'I' in an essay is unusual. This is true. Although you can use 'I' to some extent (usually when stating your answer in your introduction), you can try to make your essay seem more balanced by using other ways of stating your opinion. Let's look at some examples:

~~I think that there is too much emphasis on academic achievement in schools.~~
Academic achievement may sometimes be over emphasised in schools.
It could be said that academic achievement has too much emphasis in schools.

In the last two sentences, we are using different structures to give our opinions. In the first, we are placing the **subject** ('academic achievement') at the beginning to make the sentence **passive**, and in the second we are using a specific structure to introduce our opinion. This may seem strange, but remember that the reader knows it is your opinion, because you are writing the essay, and that your opinion comes through by what points and examples you choose to write about.

Having good reasons

Hopefully, you will be able to think of ideas and reasons for your essay. If you know that you struggle with ideas, then make sure that you start reading about common essay topics, and make a list of the ideas that you have. One good idea is to discuss these topics with other people. You'll be amazed how many people write such things as:

People who don't know about being a good citizen will become criminals.
Academic subjects are too hard for normal people.

These sentences have poor reasoning: not all people who aren't interested in being a good citizen will become criminals, and plenty of 'normal people' cope well with academic subjects.

These kinds of sentences just cannot be validated, and what you might find is that you cannot extend these into good argumentative paragraphs because there just is not enough reasoning to support them to any great extent. All of your ideas need to be explained, and sometimes it is the quality of the opinions that leads people to have a lack of ideas.

Vary your vocabulary

Remember that you are also marked on your use of vocabulary, so where you can, try to use **synonyms** instead of repeating the same words again and again. Let's look at one term in the title: *the wider demands and responsibilities involved in being a productive and positive part of society*.

We could write this in many different ways. We could use 'social responsibilities', 'social development' or 'citizenship'. We could also use longer terms such as 'learning what it means to be part of society' or 'understanding the world around us'.

If you see yourself using the same words again and again, think of other ways in which you could express the same meaning. There are of course exceptions, and these usually apply to technical or specific language for which there are no appropriate **synonyms** to use.

A good essay narrates

Lastly, remember to link your essay together well. Essentially, an essay tells a kind of story. You need to lead your reader through the argument. You can do this in a number of ways. The first is to paragraph clearly. The reader is expecting to see an introduction, two or three main body paragraphs with clear themes and a conclusion. Make sure that you have these.

Secondly, introduce what you are going to talk about in each main body paragraph. You can do this with a short sentence that presents the main point for that paragraph. Here is an example using the structure in the table in this chapter:

> *Firstly, the importance of understanding social responsibilities should not be underestimated.*

Chapter 5 – Writing

By writing a sentence such as this at the beginning of the paragraph, the reader knows we are going to present within the paragraph why it is important for children to learn about social responsibility. There should be no surprises in the paragraphs that discuss other topics.

Lastly, using linking words can also help us present our argument more clearly. These are phrases such as 'this issue', 'furthermore', 'this may result in', etc. Such phrases are like the glue to our argument. They help us connect our ideas together, and they show the reader the development of our thoughts. Try not to write sentences alone which have no connection. Look at the following examples. The first paragraph has very little connection, and will probably be marked down for that. The second paragraph connects the ideas more clearly. The connection words and phrases are underlined.

> *Firstly, the importance of understanding social responsibilities should not be underestimated. Learning about social responsibilities can give children a stronger idea of what it means to be part of a community. Learning about being a citizen can help students think of bigger issues in life; how to treat other people and how politics and the environment can affect our daily lives. Parents might not be the best source for young people to learn social responsibilities. Parents might have different views on what our part in society should involve, and not all parents might feel or be equipped to educate their children about this.*

> *<u>Firstly,</u> the importance of understanding social responsibilities should not be underestimated. Learning about social responsibilities can give children a stronger idea of what it means to be part of a community. <u>These responsibilities</u> can also help students think of bigger issues in life, <u>such as</u> how to treat others, and how politics and the environment can affect our daily lives. <u>Furthermore</u>, parents might not be the best source for young people to learn these skills, <u>because</u> not all parents are equipped to educate their children about <u>these areas</u>.*

Sample answer

Here is a sample answer to the question:

> Schools should not just teach traditional subjects like maths and language. It is also their responsibility to address the wider demands and responsibilities involved in being a productive and positive part of society.
>
> To what extent do you agree or disagree with this statement?
>
> Give reasons for your answer and include examples from your own knowledge or experience.

In many countries there is an emphasis on traditional subjects in formalised schooling rather than focusing on society and a young person's role within that society. I believe it is essential that children also learn about citizenship in schools.

Firstly, the importance of understanding social responsibilities should not be underestimated. Learning about social responsibilities can give children a stronger idea of what it means to be part of a community. These responsibilities can also help students think of bigger issues in life, such as how to treat others, and how politics and the environment can affect our daily lives. Furthermore, parents might not be the best source for young people to learn these skills, because not all parents are equipped to educate their children about these areas.

Secondly, there is already a strong focus on academic areas. It could be more beneficial if more balance were brought into these school systems, as this may mean that students who aren't academically talented realise that life is broader than merely academic knowledge. Additionally, in some countries the pressure to study traditional subjects is extremely strong. If students were given a more rounded education, this emphasis might be lessened.

However, if social responsibilities were focused on in schools, care should be taken on how this is done, as educating people about society needs to be done objectively. It may be better to have a group of academics and professionals who are known for working in social responsibility driving the syllabus development, rather than political figures.

In conclusion, formal education in schools should be broadened to include teaching on how to become a productive member of society. This could reduce the pressures of academic performance and may serve to make communities a better place in which to live.

(294 words)

Appendix 1: Listening
Audio & transcripts

Download the audio

To download the accompanying audio files, please visit:

www.prosperityeducation.net/all-about-ielts

Use the password **TIAB** to access this page. The audio file size for all five recordings is approximately 8MB.

Section 1

 Listen to the audio: Section 1

Assistant	Good afternoon, how may I help you?
Adam	I'd like a student rail card, please.
Assistant	Of course, I need to take some details from you, and then we can order the card for you.
Adam	Thanks. Can you tell me how much it is per year?
Assistant	Um, let me just check. I think the cost has increased slightly from last year. It used to be £30, but now, …. Yes, it has increased a little – it's £36 per year.
Adam	Ok.
Assistant	Right, so can I take your name, date of birth, and address?
Adam	My name's Adam Peterson.
Assistant	That's A-D-A-M Peterson, yes?
Adam	That's correct. My date of birth is the 4th of July 1998. And I live at number 110 Central Street, Brighton.

All About IELTS

Assistant	Thank you. We need your home address because the card will be sent to you in the post. But do you have an email address too? This is so I can send you a confirmation.
Adam	Um, yes ... it's a.peterson@mail.uk. So, what happens if I lose it or need to get another card next year? Do I have to call or go to a station?
Assistant	Nowadays you have to apply for a new card online. There's no need to call – just go to the new card section on the website.
Adam	Oh, that's useful. Also, can I check what the reductions on fares are with the rail card?
Assistant	On rush hour tickets, it's 10%, but on standard fares it's a 25% discount.
Adam	Wow, that's really good.
Assistant	There's just one thing I should mention – the student rail card does have a couple of restrictions besides the rush hour discount I mentioned. The most important one is that it's not valid for travel on the rapid network which serves all the country's airports. Because the airports get so busy at holiday times, discount cards can't be used.
Adam	Okay, thanks for mentioning that.
Assistant	So, you should receive your card in about a week.
Adam	That's great. Thank you.

Section 2

 Listen to the audio: Section 2

Good afternoon everyone and welcome to the tour of the theatre. Before we start the tour, I want to let you know about our afternoon activities. We have a few classes and workshops that you might be interested in. Our most popular workshop is at three o'clock, and it's about costume design. Here you'll learn about how the amazing costumes worn by our actors are made. It starts at three o'clock, and it takes place in the studio. At half past twelve you have the opportunity to read bits of Shakespeare's plays on the main stage. You'll learn how to speak in the language of the time. It's an hour long, so finishes at one thirty. And finally, there's a talk for people who are thinking of working in the theatre. It starts at half past two and goes on for an hour and a half. The talk is aimed at teenagers and young people and will cover the types of jobs and careers available in theatres. It'll take place in the learning room, which is next to the gift shop as you enter the theatre.

Right, so I just want to show you where the tour will be going. If you look at the plan on the back of your ticket, you'll see that we're at the main entrance. Our tour will start in the dressing rooms, which are on the left of the main stage. I'll tell you which rooms were used by which famous actors in the past. Then we'll go round the back of the stage so you can see more of what happens behind the scenes. I'm going to show you the changing area. This is where the actors change their costumes – I think you'll be surprised at how small it is. At the end of the tour, we'll visit the space located between the stage and the stalls. This is where the orchestra used to sit, but we don't use an orchestra anymore, so this where the sound production team are with all their amazing equipment. Right, does anyone have any questions before we start? ...

Section 3

 Listen to the audio: Section 3

Jane	Hi Mark, Hi Steph, how are you?
Mark	Fine thanks, Jane.
Stephanie	Yeah – I'm okay, what about you?
Jane	I'm good, but this term is really busy. I'm trying to organise myself as I've got a lot to do.
Mark	Oh really? I don't feel like I've got that much work this term.
Jane	Maybe that's because you didn't choose the 3D modelling module. We have to actually make an example of our design, and I'm not sure if I'll have enough time. I wish I'd chosen a module with fewer projects instead, but David is helping me, so hopefully I'll get it finished.
Stephanie	I know what you mean, Jane. That's like my innovation module. The lectures are really interesting, but Professor Jackson gives us so many articles to research afterwards. I feel like I'll never have enough time to read them all.
Mark	That sounds hard. I struggle with reading – I'm not very fast so it would be really stressful for me. For me the most difficult thing now is the planning for my final assignment. It's 15 thousand words so there's so much to think about.
Jane	Yeah, I can imagine. Look, shall we talk a bit about our robotics project? We've got a meeting with Dr. Weber next Tuesday – she'll want to know about our progress.
Stephanie	Okay. So, we should say we've decided that we don't want to design a domestic robot – you know, one that does things like vacuuming, but we want to concentrate on one that's educational.
Mark	And we should also mention that the problem we're trying to solve is communication and say that the people it's aimed at are children with disabilities.
Jane	Yes, okay. And I'd like to ask Dr Weber something. We've got to include how much we'd charge for the robot as part of the project, but I'm not sure how to do this.
Mark	Ah yeah, me neither!

Jane	So, should we ask Dr. Weber for some help?
Stephanie	Why don't we ask her for a couple of models we can use to calculate the price for the robot?
Mark	Excellent idea, Steph. Okay, well I think that's everything.
Jane	Me too. See you next week.
Stephanie	Bye

Section 4

 Listen to the audio: Section 4

Hello everyone. In today's lecture I'm going to talk about slang and how it moves from being part of a subculture to becoming part of the language. So, let's start by defining slang. It's a set of informal words and phrases which are used by a specific group of people in the same context. It could be female teenagers, football fans, or a group of office workers. It's difficult to know exactly what the origin of the word is, but it's thought to have arisen from the 16th century as a language used by criminals as a way of preventing people from being able to understand what they were talking about. Nowadays slang is much more widespread and is about being part of a social group. It's important to note that slang is the product of social forces rather than one person, which means it is difficult to know the origins of many slang words. However, this means that as slang is more widely used, these words can start to become common across many different groups – for example, words like funky and cool. These words can then be considered for entry to the dictionary. Let's now take a look at the process of how slang words enter the dictionary.

First of all, lexicographers – the people who compile dictionaries – analyse how people are using language in everyday life. They then start to make a list of possible new words to add to the dictionary based on their research. And then they must spend a long time researching these words to find out who uses them and why as well how frequently they appear in spoken and/or written language. They need to find evidence that this word is important for the modern world so that they have a lot of support for the words they want to add to the dictionary. Finally, they enlist the help of language experts to advise them on aspects of the slang words such as etymology, pronunciation, and dialect before a final decision is taken for each word. So, now I want to talk about ...

Appendix 2: Reading text

The Unluckiest Astronomer in the World?

A

The transit of Venus is one of the rarest of astronomical events. It is when Venus passes directly in front of the Sun so it can be seen against the background of the much bigger Sun. In fact, when this happens Venus looks like a small black dot moving across the Sun. Although this might not seem like an important event, it was incredibly important to astronomers in the past as it aided them in calculating the distance from the Earth to the Sun, and in turn to calculate the size of the solar system. These were also important events because of their rarity. These transits come in pairs, which are usually eight years apart, followed by long periods in between of over a hundred years. So, when the pairs come around, it's a rather special event. For example, one pair of transits happened in 1874 and 1882, and the next pair in 2004 and 2012.

B

Before these transits, the last was in 1761 and 1769. Astronomers from Britain, France and Austria dispersed around the world to gather measurements needed from a wide variety of points on Earth. One such astronomer was Frenchman Guillaume Le Gentil, who was sent to the French-controlled city of Pondicherry in India to observe the phenomenon. He set off on his journey from Paris in March 1760, a full year prior to the astronomical event, as passage to faraway places was not as easy in those days. He managed to sail to Île de France near Madagascar and then found passage on another ship heading towards Pondicherry. This ship was caught up in a monsoon and had to then travel to Africa. In 1761, with just a month left, the crew discovered that war had broken out between England and France, and that Pondicherry was now under British control. Against Le Gentil's wishes, the boat headed back to Île de France and Le Gentil missed his opportunity to observe the transit. While he managed some measurements while at sea, these were largely useless, as the movement of the ship greatly affected the accuracy of the measurements.

C

This did not deter Le Gentil, as he decided to wait the eight years necessary for the next transit to be seen, without returning to France. In these years between transits, Le Gentil mapped a proportion of the Madagascan coastline. By 1766 he decided that Manila could make a perfect observation point for this next transit. Having written to request official papers from the French Royal Academy, who had originally commissioned his voyage, he set sail again, this time for Manila. When he reached Manila and received word from the Academy that he could have diplomatic papers for his study, amazingly, authorities in Manila couldn't believe the speed at which a response came from the Academy, and he was accused of being a spy and had to return to his original plan, heading once more to Pondicherry, which had been restored into French governance.

D

Once finally at his original destination, he embarked on preparing himself for the next transit. The local government built him an observatory to his own specifications. Pondicherry had beautiful skies that were extremely clear, and in May 1769 the weather had been perfect. However, when the day of the second transit came around, the 4th of June 1769, the sky became overcast, and his view of the transit was obstructed. The weather in Manila on that day was perfect. This was a bitter blow for Le Gentil, and he started to make his way home to France. Yet again, this journey was not without its setbacks. He was delayed by illness, shipwrecks, and storms, eventually making it back to France in October 1771, 11 years after he set off on his journey.

E

The tragedy of his journey however did not end there. When he arrived home things were not as they were. Firstly, he had been declared dead by the authorities, his wife had remarried, and they had already divided up his estate between his relatives. In addition to that, he had lost his position with the French Royal Academy. He eventually found out that for many years his letters hadn't reached their destination of France due to the treacherous conditions of anything being sent by sea. He had to begin the process of trying to gain back his status as a live citizen of France, and, although in the end he achieved this, and was reinstated by the French Royal Academy, he was demoted for not obtaining the data that he set out to get. Perhaps the only redeeming outcome of this longest voyage in the history of astronomy is that he now has a small crater on the Moon named after him. Perhaps not a comforting thought for him, but nobody can deny it's deserved for such effort.

Appendix 3: WRITING
Other types of visual information

Writing Task 1
Sample question and answer – Pie chart

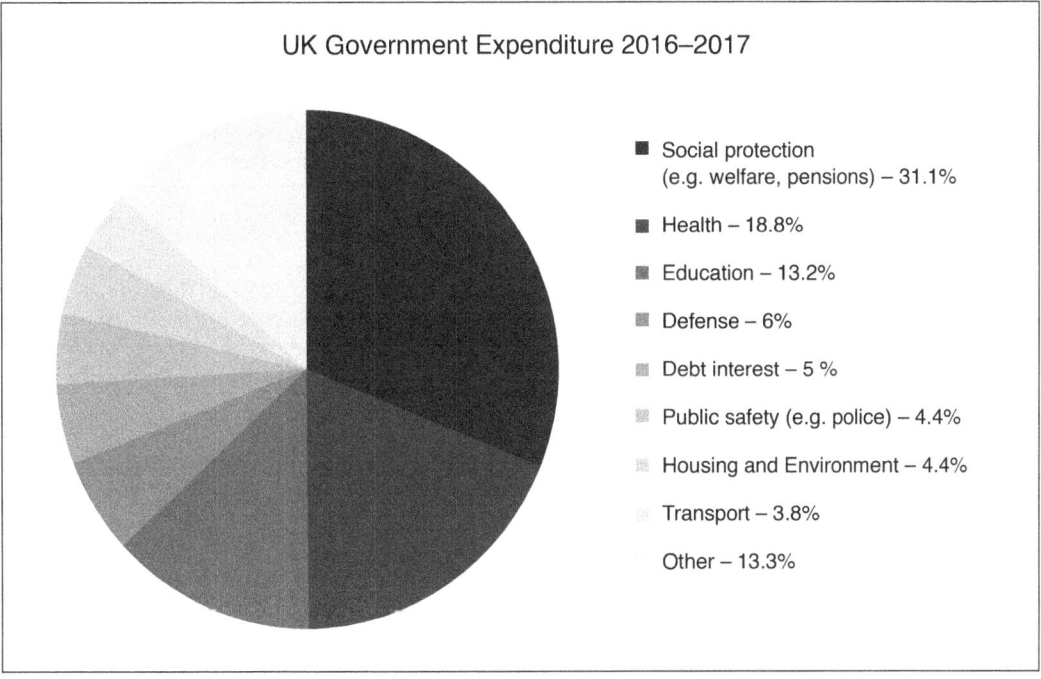

The pie chart shows how much money the government of the UK spent in the year 2016 to 2017. The chart is divided into categories and shows the spending for each one as a percentage. It can be clearly seen that some of the categories received a much higher percentage of government spending than others.

The two largest areas of government expenditure during this year were the categories of social protection, which includes money spent on pensions and the welfare of citizens, and health. The larger of these two, social protection, accounted for a third of all government spending, and health was approximately a fifth of the total. The next level of government spending includes education and 'other', both of which totalled about thirteen per cent for the year. All the other categories such as public safety, housing and the environment and transport were much lower at less than five per cent. Together these smaller categories made up roughly a quarter of all government spending for the year.

In summary, both health and social protection accounted for about half of the total government spending, while other areas were more evenly distributed.

(189 words)

Sample question and answer – Table

Tourist distribution in Kawagana (2010)								
			Origins of Tourists					
Hotel name	Tourist numbers	Percentage	European	North American	Asian	South & Central American	African	Austral-asian
Princess Hotel	78,450	19.60%	23,655	14,551	12,096	8,953	2,316	16,879
Royal Towers	118,449	29.58%	57,889	33,891	3,821	2,611	1,076	19,161
Parkview	27,245	6.81%	1,876	1,235	15,676	3,256	1,889	3,313
Mai's Palace	24,982	6.24%	2,107	1,551	15,787	3,100	1,265	1,172
West Beach	78,092	19.51%	19,167	21,872	7,945	12,787	899	15,422
Standard Inn	73,092	18.26%	17,572	15,525	11,976	10,787	950	16,282
TOTAL	400,310		122,266	88,625	67,301	41,494	8,395	72,229

The table gives information about tourists in six hotels in Kawagana in 2010. It shows the number of tourists, the percentage for each hotel, and the country of origin of the tourists. Overall, we can see that the Royal Towers hotel is the most popular, and that most tourists that visited Kawagana in 2010 came from Europe.

We can see from the table that approximately a third of tourists stayed at the Royal Towers hotel. The least popular hotels were Parkview and Mai's Place, with around six per cent of the total number of tourists. The other hotels received roughly the same amount of tourists. The majority of tourists came from Europe, North America and Australasia. Together these three regions accounted for almost three hundred *thousand tourists which was roughly three quarters of the visitors. There were far fewer tourists from other regions of the world, with the lowest number being from Africa which had fewer than 10,000 visitors to Kawagana.*

In summary, most tourists were European and North American, and the Royal Towers hotel was popular with both these groups.

(180 words)

Sample question and answer – Line graph

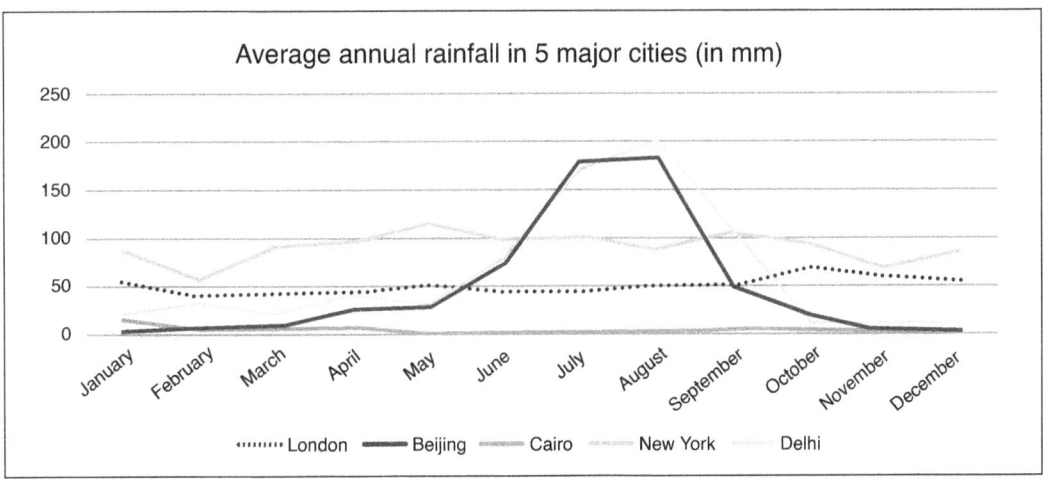

The line graph shows the average amount of rain in millimetres that falls in five cities in a year. From the graph it can be clearly seen that the rainfall in the cities differs widely through the year.

First of all, it is noticeable that the rainfall in both Beijing and Delhi is fairly similar throughout the year. Both cities start the year with low rainfall in January. This then gradually increases to about fifty millimetres in April, then a hundred in June and up to approximately two hundred millimetres in August. The rainfall for both cities peaks in August. The rainfall declines sharply from August to September and remains low for the rest of the year. In contrast, the average annual rainfall for Cairo is close to zero for the whole year. London and New York share similar rainfall patterns throughout the year. However, in London the rainfall is lower, fluctuating around fifty millimetres all year, whereas in New York it ranges between just over fifty and just over one hundred.

To summarise, while in some cities rainfall is consistent for months, other cities see massive increases in rainfall from June to October.

(194 words)

Sample question and answer – Diagram/Process

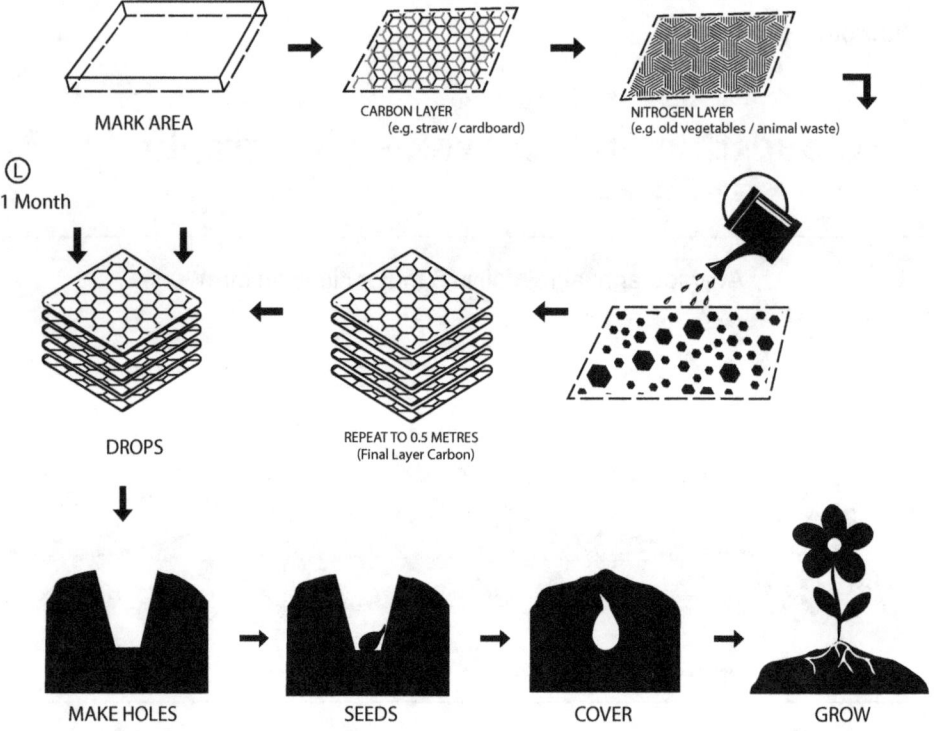

BUILDING A COMPOST FLOWER & VEGETABLE BED.

The diagram shows the process of constructing a compost bed for flowers and vegetables. The process is divided into several stages. The first set of stages includes the construction of the bed, and then the next set of stages are related to using the compost bed to help seeds grow.

First of all an area is marked out, and then several layers of carbon materials and nitrogen materials are placed on top of each other. The carbon materials could be straw or cardboard, and the nitrogen materials could be waste vegetable or animal matter. When the bed is half a metre thick it is left for one month. Then it can be used to help seeds grow. First, a hole is made, and then the bed is placed over the hole so that drips of liquid from the layers fall into the hole. Then the seeds are put into the hole and covered. The flowers or vegetables will then grow.

Overall, making a compost bed is a multi-staged process of layering materials, waiting for them to drop, and planting seeds.

(180 words)

Appendix 3 – Writing

Sample question and answer – Map/Plan

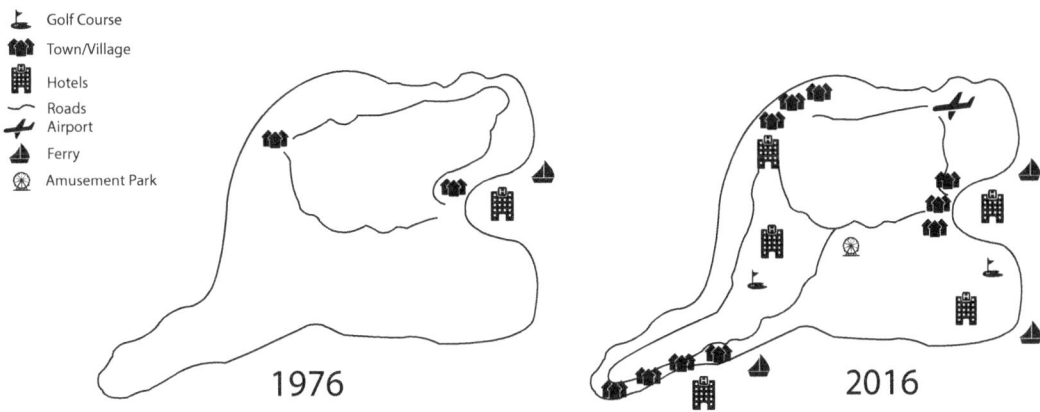

The map shows the isle of Sandforth and how it changed between the years 1976 and 2016. Overall, the map clearly shows that the island has become more developed over the forty-year period.

In 1976 the island had a small village and a town on the coast with one hotel. There was one road on the island which connected the town and the village. There was also a ferry port on the island which was located to the north of the town. At this time the rest of the island was undeveloped. By 2016 the island had changed considerably. Both the town and village had grown, and another town had appeared on the southern coast of the island. The number of hotels had increased, and two more roads had been constructed. By 2016 there was also an airport, two golf courses, and an amusement park.

It can be seen that the isle of Sandforth is now much more highly developed compared to 1976.

(164 words)

Glossary & index

Active (form): In an active sentence the subject does the action, e.g. *My teacher marked my essay.* Compare with a passive sentence where the subject receives the action, e.g. *My essay was marked by my teacher.*   20, 40

Adjective: A word which describes a noun or a pronoun, e.g. *large, expensive, positive.*   12, 42

Article: *a/an, the.*   15, 23

Chronological: Things which are in the order that they happen.   43

Common European Framework of Reference (CEFR): An international system for standardising language ability.   31

Comparative: An adjective or adverb which describes a difference, e.g. *thinner, more quickly, better.*   29

Conclusion: The end or final section of a piece of writing such as an essay.   64, 67

Conditional (form): A sentence with two halves where one depends on the other, e.g. *If I get a bonus, I'll buy a new car.*   29, 34

Connected speech: The ways in which words are connected in a stream of spoken language.   22

Counter-argument: An idea or argument which opposes another argument.   67

Criteria / Criterion: A standard or rule which is used to evaluate the quality of something.   31, 57

Descriptor: A phrase which explains how to achieve each level or grade in a test.   31, 57

Deviate: To do something differently from what is usual or expected.   68

Discursive: Something which involves discussion.   6

Distraction: Something which moves your attention from one thing to another thing.   13

Glossary & Index

Distractor: An option in a multiple-choice question which is not the correct answer. — 13

Hypothesis / Hypothesise: A possible reason or explanation for something based on ideas. — 31, 32

Hypothetical: Based on something which is reasoned from an idea. — 34

Idiomatic expressions: A phrase where the meaning of all the words together is different from the individual meanings of the words. — 29

Introduction: The beginning or first section of a piece of writing such as an essay. — 64, 67

Inversion and emphatic structures: A grammatical structure which switches the subject and verb for emphasis, e.g. *Had I known you were out, I wouldn't have called.* — 29

Language buff: A person who is very interested in and/or knowledgeable about languages. — 32

Lexical / Lexically: Connected with the words of a language rather than the grammar. — 21

Linking words: Words which connect ideas together, e.g. *however, in addition, for example.* — 71

Low-frequency words/ low-frequency vocabulary: Words which we don't use often. — 11, 41, 52

Main body: The middle section or paragraphs in a piece of writing such as an essay. — 59, 67

Main features: The important parts of something. — 55, 61

Modal: A modal is a verb that helps add information to a main verb, such as 'can', 'should' or 'might'. — 34, 64

Monologue: When only one person is speaking. — 6, 12

Noun: A word which describes an object, a person, or a place. — 12, 16, 23, 41, 42

Paragraph: A section of writing which contains one idea or topic and is separated by space above and below it.   16, 40, 45, 57

Paraphrasing: To repeat the same writing in speech or writing using different words but keeping the original meaning.   19, 21, 42

Passive (form): In a passive sentence the subject receives the action, e.g. *My essay was marked by my teacher.* Compare with an active sentence where the subject does the action, e.g. *My teacher marked my essay.*   20, 23, 34, 43, 69

Past participle: A verb form which often ends in –ed and forms some tenses, e.g. I've worked here for five years.   43

Plural: More than one of something, e.g. *cars, women, studies*.   49, 52

Prepositions: Small words used to show the relationship between things, e.g. *We'll do it after dinner, The box is under the bed, I left my phone at home.*   61

Proficiency: The level of language a person has is known as their language proficiency.   5, 8

Subject (grammatical): The subject of a sentence is the noun (thing or idea) that the sentence is about. It often begins the sentence.   46, 69

Summary / Summarise: A brief outline of the main points or features of something.   16, 45, 55, 59

Superlatives: Adjectives or adverbs which describe the highest degree of something, e.g. *thinnest, most quickly, the best.*   29

Synonyms: Words which have similar meanings.   31, 41, 44, 47, 57, 70

Tenses: A construction of a verb that indicates the time the action took place e.g. You are reading a book. I went shopping yesterday.   29, 43, 58, 60

Transactional: Relating to the exchange of information to achieve an aim (such as open a bank account, book a holiday, pay for something).   6, 12

Verb: An action or state word (e.g. run, be, look, think).   16, 45

Glossary & Index

Verb combinations: Where more than one verb is used consecutively in a sentence e.g. I stopped smoking last year. — 29

Vowel: The letters *a, e, i, o,* and *u.* — 22

Weak forms: Unstressed sounds used in speech. — 22

All About IELTS

IELTS Reading Practice: Academic Student Book

Each of the 14 units introduces a different reading task that you may encounter during the IELTS Academic Reading test:

1. Matching headings
2. True / False / Yes / No / Not Given
3. Matching information
4. Summary completion
5. Sentence completion
6. Multiple choice
7. Matching features
8. Choosing a title
9. Categorisation/classification
10. Matching sentence endings
11. Table completion
12. Flowchart completion
13. Diagram completion
14. Short answer questions

Each unit contains three two-page sections:

1. **Think and prepare** starts with some questions to get you thinking about the unit topic, and introduces some challenging words and phrases that will appear in the practice activities that follow.

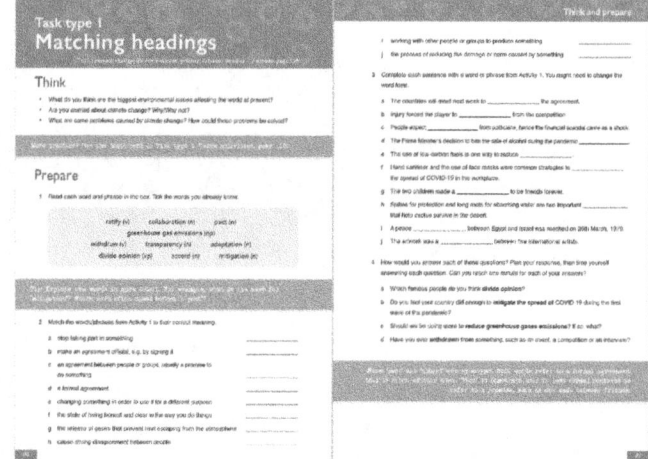

2. **Practise** introduces a new reading task for you to practise the task type using a text that is shorter than what will feature in the exam. It starts with some strategies and tips for how to approach each task, for you to try these strategies out during the activities then reflect on what went well, what you learned and what you will need to do to improve.

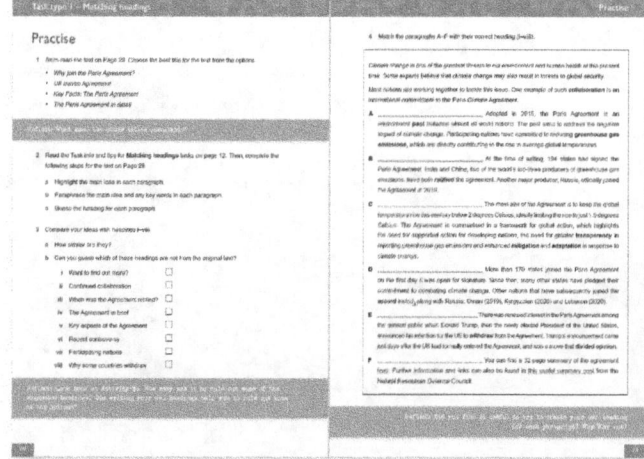

3. **Put it to the test** includes a text that is designed to replicate an IELTS Reading test task. There is no support here – it's just you, the text and the questions!

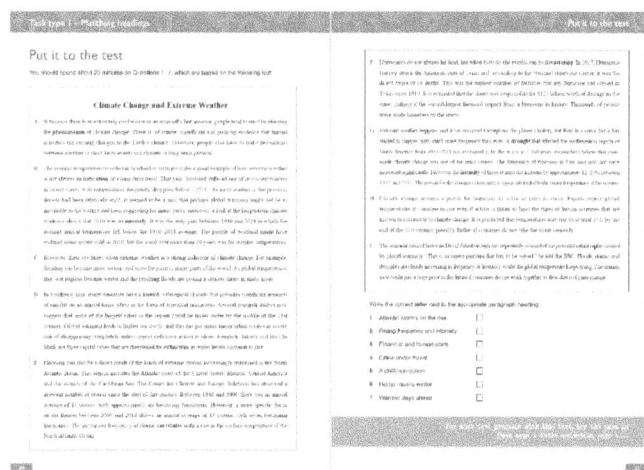

Appendices:

Task info and tips:
Definitions of each task type, and tips on how to approach the task.

Extra activities:
Further practice in applying different task types to the units' texts.

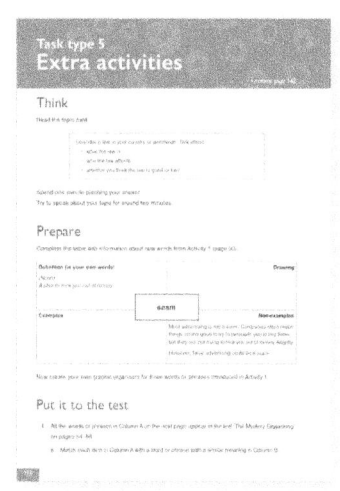

Answers:
Comprehensive answers and guidance for each activity.

Glossary and Index:
Definitions of all high-level vocabulary used.

All About IELTS

IELTS Reading Practice: Academic Sample Papers

Each of the 8 exam-styled tests includes the different reading tasks that you may encounter during the IELTS Academic Reading test:

1. Matching headings
2. True / False / | Yes / No / Not Given
3. Matching information
4. Summary completion
5. Sentence completion
6. Multiple choice
7. Matching features
8. Choosing a title
9. Categorisation/classification
10. Matching sentence endings
11. Table completion
12. Flowchart completion
13. Diagram completion
14. Short answer questions

Each test contains 3 texts and 40 questions.

The content has been written to closely replicate the IELTS exam experience, and has undergone comprehensive expert and peer review.

Author Jane Turner is an associate lecturer in EAP/EFL at Anglia Ruskin University, Cambridge, and an EFL materials writer for international exam boards, universities and publishers. She previously worked as a Cambridge ESOL examiner for the British Council, and holds an MA in Education Management, and Cambridge CELTA and DELTA.

IELTS Academic Reading Practice

Sample Papers

Jane Turner

PROSPERITY EDUCATION

All About IELTS

READING PASSAGE 1

You should spend about 20 minutes on Questions 1–14, which are based on Reading Passage 1 on the next page.

Questions 1–5
Reading Passage 1 has 6 sections, A–F.
Choose the correct headings for Sections *A* and *C–F* from the list of headings below.
Write the correct number i–viii in answer boxes 1–5.

List of headings
i   Detecting lies and opportunities
ii   The development of olfaction
iii Smelling for survival
iv   Trends in perfume making
v   Smell and memory
vi   The impact of smell in retail
vii The science behind creating popular scents
viii The complexity of smell

Example:

                Answer

1 Section B   *iii*

1 Section A

2 Section C

3 Section D

4 Section E

5 Section F

The Sense of Smell

Section A
Although we may take it for granted, our ability to smell, also called olfaction, has played a crucial role in human evolution. Olfaction enabled early humans to identify food sources, and differentiate between safe things to eat and those which were potentially harmful. Smell also helps reinforce vital blood bonds. Research has shown that humans develop an innate olfactory instinct within the womb. Unborn babies become familiar with the unique smell of their mother, meaning that when born, they can distinguish their caregiver from other adults. Likewise, mothers can instinctively recognise the so-called "odour cues" of their own baby. As a result, when faced with similar-looking infants, parents can identify their own offspring, thereby ensuring the safety of their baby. Would the human race have flourished as it has without olfaction?

Section B
In addition to detecting actual scents or odours, smell is the sense often associated with identifying hidden threats to our wellbeing. We don't literally use our nose to discover whether someone is being dishonest. Rather, we often refer to our feelings of suspicion or mistrust in smell-related terms, as the expression "to smell a rat" illustrates. Likewise, the idiom "smell blood" is used when we sense an opportunity to take advantage of someone we believe is in a weak position. Similar expressions exist in many other languages, suggesting that, compared to other senses, we may have a more emotional or even instinctive relationship with smell. This is just one aspect that arguably makes olfaction the most mysterious of the five senses.

Section C
Of course, humans now employ multiple senses when interacting with the world. In fact, much emphasis is now placed on sight and sound. Far more scientific research is conducted into these two senses, and, consequently, more is known about them. However, smell is far from being an inferior sense. For one thing, our sense of taste depends heavily on olfaction. What's more, although smell is one of the oldest of the five senses, it is far from the simplest. Our ancient sense of smell has always been remarkably sophisticated. For instance, while our eyes have just four light sensors to sense visual stimuli, the nose uses approximately four hundred different olfactory receptors. Such a large number of highly sensitive receptors enables the nose to identify an astonishing range of scents. In fact, researchers now believe that humans are capable of detecting at least a trillion different smells.

Section D
There are further differences between smell and other senses, especially in the way olfactory information is received and processed in the brain. Information about touch, sight or sound initially enters the brain through an area called the thalamus. However, smells are directly processed in a different area called the olfactory bulb, situated by the hippocampus. This area of the brain is involved in learning, long-term memory and emotion, and is necessary for remembering past events and experiences. The fact that only olfactory signals are processed near the hippocampus could indicate that smells are processed on a deeper, more emotional level compared to other types of sensory information. Some experts believe that recalling past experiences from sights or sounds leads to factual types of response. By contrast, odours can create intense emotional reactions, almost as if the smell transports us directly back to the past. This "smell nostalgia" can produce incredibly powerful feelings in us, especially if the memory is associated with someone we haven't seen for a long time.

Section E
The power of smell can even be exploited for commercial gain. One study found that shoppers may spend up to twenty minutes longer in a shop that smells nice, and that pleasant scents could increase the probability of a sale by up to eighty per cent on average. Similarly, the associations we have for certain scents can be used to make people feel certain emotions. That's why baking is a common tactic used when people are trying to sell their home. When potential buyers come to view the property, the smell of baking coming from the kitchen not only makes the home smell nice, but also conveys a sense of cosiness. Subconsciously, people entering the home will make the association with the pleasant scents and positive feelings about the property itself. This can make all the difference in property sales.

Section F
Then there is the perfume sector, which continues to see huge growth. One of the latest innovations has been the development of aromatherapy perfumes designed to enhance one's mood. What's more, luxury fashion houses can attract new customers by developing their own scents. Many consumers want to buy something associated with designer fashion without having to worry about the price. And just like clothing trends, specific perfume ingredients or perfume styles become fashionable at certain points in time. However, unlike clothing, perfume smells slightly different on every person. We all have our own unique skin chemistry, which means that the various ingredients in the perfume react in different ways on our skin. For this reason, no company has managed to create a scent with universal appeal. This again demonstrates our special relationship with smell.

All About IELTS

Questions 6–11
Do the following statements agree with the claims of the writer in Reading Passage 1?

In boxes 6–11, write:

> **TRUE** If the statement agrees with the information in the passage
> **FALSE** If the statement contradicts the information in the passage
> **NOT GIVEN** If there is no information on this in the passage

6 Humans' sense of smell starts to develop as soon as they are born.

7 Olfaction receives less academic attention than some other senses.

8 It is impossible to detect different smells without using taste receptors.

9 Sensory signals about smells and sounds are sent to different parts of the brain.

10 Visual memories produce stronger emotional responses than olfactory memories.

11 The use of smell can influence the average amount of money customers spend in shops.

Questions 12–14
*Answer the questions below using **NO MORE THAN THREE WORDS** from the passage for each answer.*

Write your answers in boxes 12–14.

12 Which phrase is mentioned as an idiom that is used to express a sense of doubt?

13 What is the minimum number of smells that experts believe the human nose can detect?

14 Which part of the brain is associated with remembering past events?

READING PASSAGE 2

You should spend about 20 minutes on Questions 15–27, which are based on Reading Passage 2 below.

Section A
Commercial farming has seen numerous changes over the years. For instance, agricultural innovations have made farming less labour-intensive, with tasks such as watering and planting crops becoming increasingly mechanised. Likewise, pest management has been transformed with the introduction of chemical pesticides and the development of genetically modified crops. While such developments have helped farms to increase crop yields, food security remains a key concern. Given the rising global population, farmers are struggling to meet the growing demand for affordable, safe produce. At the same time, the environmental impact of agriculture is under closer scrutiny than ever before.

Section B
Agriculture puts a strain on the environment in several ways. Farming requires a substantial amount of land, an issue of global importance as land becomes ever scarcer. Agriculture typically contributes to other important problems, too, such as soil erosion, loss of wildlife habitats and pollution. Environmentalists also point out that the carbon footprint of many forms of agriculture is considerable, as are the energy and water requirements of farming. For these reasons, scientists and growers strive to identify more ecologically sustainable ways to supply the world with fresh food.

Section C
In recent decades, the quest for environmentally friendly farming practices has largely centred on growing crops in town and cities. The development of vertical farming has played an important role in this. As the name suggests, this type of farming involves growing crops in vertical racks or shelves stacked on top of one another rather than planting them horizontally across wide open spaces. Vertical farms maximise urban space by making use of abandoned sites such as vacant apartment blocks, disused underground tunnels, abandoned mine shafts or old shipping containers. While vertical farming is still relatively new, its value has risen sharply. This market is forecast to be worth almost £10 billion within a decade.

Section D
Growing vertically is just one aspect that sets this form of farming apart from conventional agriculture. Another is that the crops are grown without soil. This can be done using a hydroponic growing method, where plants are grown in large trays or containers connected to a large water tank. Instead of taking nutrients from soil, the plants are fed a liquid solution. Using a water pump, the liquid is sent from the water tank into the containers at certain intervals, often regulated by an automatic timer. The liquid solution contains the essential nutrients needed for plant growth. Submerging only the roots of the plant in the solution prevents the plants from suffering damage from excess water. Once the container is full, the solution will overflow and drain back into the tank. The liquid remains there until the timer automatically activates the pump again. Thus, the mineral solution is circulated between the tank and the plant tray. The mineral composition of the solution can be adjusted to ensure plants receive the right amounts of nutrients.

Section E
Of course, plants also need light. In vertical farming, the crops are grown indoors and therefore have limited access to natural light. Therefore, artificial lighting must be used, and arranged in such a way that it can reach every layer of the plants. Placing a single powerful light source directly above the highest layer of plants could result in the top plants being overexposed to harsh light, while the trays of plants beneath them receive insufficient light. Fortunately, with advances in lighting technology, individual lighting units can be placed safely between each layer of plants. This ensures that all plants receive adequate light. In fact, modern LED lighting can be adjusted to generate lighting of different colours and intensity, meaning that it's possible to optimise the lighting specifically for each individual type of crop. Experts argue that this leads to greater control over when the plants flower and even how the crops will taste.

Section F
Clearly, vertical farming makes use of ingenious techniques, and its growing number of supporters argue that it's vital for securing a sustainable food supply. Vertical farming is also relatively efficient in terms of its water requirements, meaning that far less water is used to grow plants. This is an important ecological advantage. In addition, since the crops are grown in areas where they don't have to travel so far to reach their end user, it's argued that this reduces the carbon footprint of agriculture. On top of this, the crop yields achieved by vertical farming methods are impressive, often beating those achieved by conventional farming. For example, one study found that twenty times more lettuce can be grown in vertical farms than in fields. Viewed from the perspective of the planet's diminishing land resources, this is an undeniable benefit, and one that is likely to become increasingly important.

Section G
Investment in vertical-farming technology is increasing. Nevertheless, claims that vertical farming is set to revolutionise agriculture may be a little premature. Unless the expense required to create vertical farms falls, it will remain too costly for most growers. This will prevent vertically farmed produce from being easily affordable. Moreover, many of the world's most popular crops cannot be grown easily using vertical farms. And while vertical farming does offer several ecological benefits, its green credentials can be disputed because of its extremely high energy consumption. Some of these obstacles may eventually be overcome, but it's unlikely that vertical farming will replace conventional farming entirely.

Questions 15–22
Reading Passage 2 has 7 paragraphs labelled A–G.
Which paragraph contains the following information?

Write the correct letter **A–G** in answer boxes 15–22.

NB: You may use any letter more than once.

15 evidence that vertical farms can produce high quantities of food

16 a financial prediction about the growth of the vertical-farming sector

17 an example of how a practical problem associated with vertical farming has been resolved

18 a description of how traditional farming can negatively impact nature.

19 an economic argument against vertical farming

20 a description of the locations used for vertical farming

21 an example of how scientific innovation has helped farmers protect their crops

22 a common method of feeding plants in vertical-farming systems

Questions 23–26
Complete the flow chart below.

Choose **NO MORE THAN TWO WORDS** from the text for each answer.
Write your answers in gaps 23–26.

Vertical farming: A hydroponic system

In a hydroponic system, crops can be grown without using
(23)_____.

↓

Instead, plants are grown in containers that receive water from a
(24)_____.

↓

A liquid is regularly pumped into the containers. This solution contains
(25)_____ that help plants grow well.

↓

Since only the roots are in contact with the solution, the harmful effects
of **(26)**_____ are avoided.

Question 27
Choose the correct letter, A, B, C, D, or E.
Which of the following is the most suitable title for Reading Passage 2?

Write the correct letter **A–E** in the answer box below.

A   How technology has helped make vertical farms more popular

B   Is vertical farming the key to sustainable food supplies?

C   Water and energy consumption in vertical farming

D   The practical limitations of vertical farming

E   How have vertical farms transformed urban environments?

READING PASSAGE 3

You should spend about 20 minutes on **Questions 28–40**, which are based on Reading Passage 3 below.

New Directions: *Rita Lewis on the marvels of maps*

I've always been fascinated with maps. As a child, I spent hours exploring world atlases memorising the exotic names of all the faraway places that caught my imagination. I was intrigued by the tiny dots of remote islands, and imagined how long it would take to sail to such places, and what I might find there. As an adult, my interest in maps has become more practical. I use them as tools for planning holidays or days out. Maps showing the elevations of hills help me to identify suitable walking routes, while city maps highlight places of local interest. While I've always been curious about maps, only recently has my attention turned towards cartography.

The fact that early humans depicted their surroundings in cave paintings proves we've always sought to understand the physical world. In this sense, maps have existed for millennia. Some ancient maps showed the night sky rather than land features, presumably for navigational purposes. The first published world map is thought to have been the work of the ancient Greek philosopher Anaximander. While he is regarded as the "father of cartography", ancient Chinese cartographers were just as influential. They developed maps with gridlines and scales, which remains an important aspect of modern mapmaking. Jewish cartographers also played an important role by developing charts for navigation at sea. Cartography also owes much to individuals including Piri Reis, Al Idrisi and Fra Mauro. They mapped much of the world and set the foundations of the modern discipline.

It's incredible to think that much of our knowledge about the Earth was discovered using only simple instruments and handmade maps. For centuries, distances were calculated using ropes or chains of specific lengths. Over time, the development of basic instruments and tools helped cartographers and explorers to make their calculations with greater ease. For instance, compasses allowed cartographers to plot angles. Later, the introduction of small telescopes or magnifying glasses attached to these compasses made it easier to see two points that were far apart. Of course, compared with modern maps, many old maps were less detailed. However, given the fact that they were made without the aid of sophisticated digital tools, some of the most ancient maps in existence are remarkably accurate.

We shouldn't assume that inaccuracies on historical maps are the result of miscalculations. Sometimes cartographers intentionally misrepresented geographical features for valid scientific purposes. For instance, in the sixteenth century, the cartographer Gerardus Mercator produced a map which became known as the Mercator projection. As the map was designed to serve as a navigational tool for sailors, Mercator altered the shape and scale of the continents. He did this to make it easier to represent the curved shape of the world on a flat map. This enabled sailors to plot sea routes more easily. The Mercator projection has been extremely influential for centuries and while it isn't perfectly precise, it's still widely used.

Maps from the past also provide us with fascinating insights into the development of our world. Rather than showing physical geographical features like mountains or rivers, political maps focus on features of human geography, such as official boundaries or road systems. Such details can quickly become outdated through no fault of the cartographer. Therefore, such maps shouldn't be viewed as fixed representations of reality, but as records of how the world has been organised at certain points in history. Maps can reveal how the world was once perceived. For instance, ancient European maps often featured artistic elements and symbolic imagery. These illustrations were visual commentaries conveying positive or negative viewpoints about various places. This form of "cartographic propaganda" demonstrates that there is more to maps than geographic fact.

The role of maps extends far beyond presenting technical information in a systematic way. Anyone who has ever seen a beautiful, hand-drawn ancient map would surely accept that cartography's position on the art–science spectrum is open to debate. Cartographers have to keep in mind their intended audience, and the purpose of the product. Much like a cookbook, maps may be used to entertain and inspire as well as inform. Therefore, cartographers should consider not only geographical information, but also ease of use and attractive presentation. Thus, cartography incorporates both scientific and aesthetic elements.

Mapmaking continues to be a highly specialist field, combining technical skill, subject knowledge and an eye for detail. Of course, the mapmaking process has inevitably moved with the times. Modern cartographers have cutting-edge technology at their disposal, helping them to create maps which are as precise as possible. Thanks to digital mapping tools, maps now cover even greater detail than ever. For this reason, the days of struggling with a paper map in the wind and rain may soon be over, as we can consult maps directly on our phones. As this technology becomes widespread, people now entering the mapmaking profession are expected to be familiar with programming languages. Scientific innovations are also used to identify physical changes on the planet. For instance, as the consequences of climate change start to affect the Earth, satellite imaging is playing a key role in helping cartographers to identify areas where maps need to be altered. Unquestionably, mapmaking remains vital.

Questions 28–34
Choose the correct letter, A, B, C or D.
Write the correct letter **A–D** in answer boxes 28–34.

28 What does the writer say about her experience of maps?

   A   Looking at maps has inspired her to visit unusual places.

   B   She prefers studying cartography to looking at maps.

   C   Over time, her main reason to look at maps has changed.

   D   Her knowledge of the world is mainly due to looking at maps.

29 What contribution did early Chinese cartographers make to mapmaking?

   A   They created a mathematical system of organising places on maps.

   B   They produced the first complete maps of the entire world.

   C   They produced the earliest examples of navigational maps.

   D   They invented new instruments to produce maps.

30 In the past, cartographers used to measure the distance between points using a

   A   telescope.

   B   chain.

   C   compass.

   D   magnifying glass.

31 What point does the writer make about Mercator's maps?

   A   Mercator's maps led sailors to make more mistakes.

   B   Mercator knew there was inaccurate information in his maps.

   C   Mercator made errors when calculating how big continents were.

   D   Mercator's maps have become less popular nowadays.

32 Political maps are an example of maps which

    A   can be interpreted in different ways.

    B   are designed to change people's attitudes about a place.

    C   combine geographic and artistic features.

    D   may go out of date over time.

33 The writer refers to the example of cookbooks to show that

    A   the purpose of a publication may affect how it is presented.

    B   there is little difference between art and science.

    C   it is important to present technical information clearly.

    D   artistic elements can improve the quality of a factual publication.

34 According to the text, satellite technology is particularly useful for

    A   discovering new areas that need to be mapped.

    B   making the mapmaking process more efficient.

    C   correcting mathematical errors on earlier maps.

    D   updating maps due to environmental changes.

Questions 35–40
Complete the sentences below with words taken from Reading Passage 3.
Use **NO MORE THAN TWO WORDS** for each answer.

Write your answers in boxes 35–40.

35 Early navigational maps depicted the ...

36 Some charts that helped sailors navigate were originally created by ...

37 A design that made it easier to represent the Earth's round shape on flat maps was the ...

38 Using map design to influence people's opinions is a type of …

39 There are different opinions about whether cartography should be categorised as science or …

40 Working as a cartographer now requires knowledge of …

www.ingramcontent.com/pod-product-compliance
Lightning Source LLC
Chambersburg PA
CBHW081353080526
44588CB00016B/2480